Environmentalism sin

'A lucid, concise, and balanced survey of modern environmentalism as it evolved in the US, UK, and the international NGO movement.'
Professor John R. McNeill, *Georgetown University*, USA

'This is a wonderful introductory text to the wide field of environmentalism. The history of this field is unpacked in a logical, systematic and engaging fashion and the content will inform the lay and interested person.'
Dr Phia Steyn, *University of Stirling*, UK

Today environmental issues are part of daily life, a feature of the modern world almost everyone now recognises. Contemporary environmentalism has promoted a way of speaking and thinking about the environment that was not possible or imaginable decades ago.

Environmentalism since 1945 provides a concise introduction to the greening of politics, science, economics and culture in the post-war period. It covers key issues, including:

- the birth of the environmental movement
- development of global environmental governance
- climate science and the rise of climate scepticism
- Green New Deal and the call for prosperity without growth
- greening of mainstream culture and efforts to change attitudes and behaviour
- challenges the environmental movement will have to address to continue to be a force for change.

Each chapter provides a historical perspective, anchoring topics to real events, influential ideas and prominent figures. This book is an essential introduction for all those interested in the history of environmentalism.

Gary Haq is a Human Ecologist and Senior Research Associate at the Stockholm Environment Institute at the University of York, UK.

Alistair Paul is a Senior Policy Advisor at the UK Department of Energy and Climate Change and former Senior Research Associate at the Stockholm Environment Institute.

The Making of the Contemporary World
Edited by Eric J. Evans and Ruth Henig

The Making of the Contemporary World series provides challenging interpretations of contemporary issues and debates within strongly defined historical frameworks. The range of the series is global, with each volume drawing together material from a range of disciplines – including economics, politics and sociology. The books in this series present compact, indispensable introductions for students studying the modern world.

Asylum Seekers and Refugees in the Contemporary World
David J. Whittaker

China and the World since 1945
Chi-kwan Mark

China Under Communism
Alan Lawrence

The Cold War
David Painter

Communism and its Collapse
Stephen White

Conflict and Reconciliation in the Contemporary World
David J. Whittaker

Conflicts in the Middle East since 1945
Beverley Milton-Edwards and Peter Hinchcliffe

Decolonization
Raymond Betts

Dividing and Uniting Germany
J. K. A. Thomaneck and Bill Niven

The Extreme Right in Western Europe
Paul Hainsworth

International Economic Relations since 1945
Catherine R. Schenk

The International Economy since 1945
Sidney Pollard

Islamic Fundamentalism since 1945
Beverley Milton-Edwards

Latin America
John Ward

Pacific Asia
Yumei Zhang

The Soviet Union in World Politics
Geoffrey Roberts

Southern Africa
Jonathan Farley

States and Nationalism in Europe Since 1945
Malcolm Anderson

Terrorists and Terrorism in the Contemporary World
David J. Whittaker

Thatcher and Thatcherism
Eric J. Evans

United Nations in the Contemporary World
David J. Whittaker

The Uniting of Europe
Stanley Henig

US Foreign Policy since 1945
Alan P. Dobson and Steve Marsh

Women and Political Power in Europe since 1945
Ruth Henig and Simon Henig

Environmentalism since 1945

Gary Haq and Alistair Paul

LONDON AND NEW YORK

First published 2012
by Routledge
2 Park Square, Milton Park, Abingdon, Oxon OX14 4RN

Simultaneously published in the USA and Canada
by Routledge
711 Third Avenue, New York, NY 10017

Routledge is an imprint of the Taylor & Francis Group, an informa business

© 2012 Gary Haq and Alistair Paul

The right of Gary Haq and Alistair Paul to be identified as authors of this work has been asserted by them in accordance with sections 77 and 78 of the Copyright, Designs and Patents Act 1988.

All rights reserved. No part of this book may be reprinted or reproduced or utilised in any form or by any electronic, mechanical, or other means, now known or hereafter invented, including photocopying and recording, or in any information storage or retrieval system, without permission in writing from the publishers.

Trademark notice: Product or corporate names may be trademarks or registered trademarks, and are used only for identification and explanation without intent to infringe.

British Library Cataloguing in Publication Data
A catalogue record for this book is available from the British Library

Library of Congress Cataloging-in-Publication Data
Haq, Gary.
Environmentalism since 1945 / Gary Haq and Alistair Paul.
p. cm. -- (Making of the contemporary world)
Includes bibliographical references.
1. Environmentalism--United States--History. 2. Environmental policy--United States--History. 3. Green movement--United States--History. I. Paul, Alistair. II. Title.
GE180.H36 2011
333.720973--dc22
2011010785

ISBN: 978-0-415-60181-8 (hbk)
ISBN: 978-0-415-60182-5 (pbk)
ISBN: 978-0-203-80387-5 (ebk)

Typeset in Times New Roman
by Taylor & Francis Books

Printed and bound in Great Britain by the MPG Books Group

For our children

Sophia Jasmine Haq (2009–10)

Patrick Storm Allott (b. 31 December 2010)

Contents

Acronyms and abbreviations ix
Historical timeline of environmentalism xi
Acknowledgements xvii

1 Introduction 1

The environmental idea 1
Scope of the book 2

2 The environmental movement 5

Early environmental campaigns 5
Dawn of a new movement 7
US environmental successes 8
European mobilisation 9
Global environmental campaigns 11
A new wave of grassroots movements 13
A global counterculture 16
Contemporary campaign challenges 18
A crowded marketplace 18
Tackling climate change 21
Understanding the environmental movement 24

3 Global environmental governance 26

Resource security and sovereignty 26
UN Conference on the Human Environment 28
Environment and development 29
The Rio Earth Summit 31
Instruments of global environmental governance 34
Global climate change policy 36
Understanding global environmental governance 39

4 Science and the environment — 41

The study of nature 41
The control of nature 43
Radical ecology 45
Science in environmental policy 47
The burden of proof 49
Science under fire 53
Understanding science and the environment 57

5 Economics and the environment — 58

Early economic thought 58
Economic growth and production 60
The birth of ecological economics 64
Valuing nature 65
Privatising common resources 68
A Global Green New Deal 70
Understanding economics and the environment 72

6 Popular culture and environment — 75

The post-war consumer boom 75
From Earthrise to Earth Day 77
Taking action 78
The rise of the green consumer 80
Greening the mainstream 83
Changing public attitudes 87
Changing individual behaviour 89
Understanding popular culture and the environment 90

7 The future of environmentalism — 92

Environmental progress and change 93
Environmental scepticism 94
The role of technology 95
Winning hearts and minds 96
Post-environmentalism 97
A new age of environmental localism 98

Notes — 100
Further reading — 114
Index — 116

Acronyms and abbreviations

CBD	Convention on Biological Diversity
CFC	chlorofluorocarbon
CITES	Convention on International Trade in Endangered Species of Wild Fauna and Flora
CND	Campaign for Nuclear Disarmament
COP	Conference of the Parties
CPRE	Campaign to Protect Rural England
CRU	Climatic Research Unit
CSD	Commission on Sustainable Development
DDD	dichlorodiphenyldichloroethane
DDT	dichlorodiphenyltrichloroethane
EDF	Environmental Defense Fund
EU	European Union
FAO	Food and Agriculture Organization
FDA	Food and Drink Administration (US)
FoE	Friends of the Earth
GARP	Global Atmospheric Research Programme
GDP	gross domestic product
GEF	Global Environment Facility
GEMS	Global Environment Monitoring System
GGND	Global Green New Deal
GM	genetically modified
GNP	gross national product
IMF	International Monetary Fund
IPPC	Intergovernmental Panel on Climate Change
IUCN	International Union for Conservation of Nature
KAB	Keep America Beautiful
MDGs	Millennium Development Goals
MEA	multilateral environmental agreement
MIT	Massachusetts Institute of Technology

NASA	National Aeronautics and Space Administration (US)
NEPAD	New Partnership for Africa's Development
NGO	non-governmental organisation
NRDC	Natural Resources Defense Council
OECD	Organisation for Economic Co-operation and Development
OPEC	Organization of the Petroleum Exporting Countries
RSPB	Royal Society for the Protection of Birds
SSE	steady-state economy
UEA	University of East Anglia
UN	United Nations
UNCED	UN Conference on Environment and Development
UNCHE	UN Conference on the Human Environment
UNEP	UN Environment Programme
UNESCO	UN Educational, Scientific and Cultural Organization
UNFCCC	UN Framework Convention on Climate Change
UNSCCUR	UN Scientific Conference on the Conservation and Utilization of Resources
WCED	World Commission on Environment and Development
WEHAB	water and sanitation, energy, health, agriculture and biodiversity
WHO	World Health Organization
WMO	World Meteorological Organization
WSSD	World Summit on Sustainable Development
WTO	World Trade Organization
WWF	World Wide Fund for Nature

Historical timeline of environmentalism

1945	The Second World War ends
	The United Nations is established
1948	Fairfield Osborn publishes *Our Plundered Planet*
	William Vogt publishes *Road to Survival*
1947	The US Defenders of Wildlife is established
	The US Marshall Plan for post-war economic recovery is adopted
1949	UN Scientific Conference on Conservation and Utilization of Resources (UNSCCUR) is held in New York
	Aldo Leopold publishes *A Sand County Almanac*
1951	The US Nature Conservancy is established
	US President Truman establishes the Paley Commission to examine future supply of natural resources
1952	The great London smog kills an estimated 12,000 people
	The Paley Commission publishes *Resources for Freedom* report
1953	The Keep America Beautiful campaign is established
	The Coronation of Queen Elizabeth II takes place in London
1954	The UK Beaver Committee concludes levels of air pollution can no longer be tolerated
	Food rationing ends in the UK
1955	First UK Independent Television channel (ITV) is launched
1956	UK adopts its first Clean Air Act
1957	A fire occurs at Britain's Windscale nuclear power plant
1958	US economist J. K. Galbraith publishes *The Affluent Society*
1961	World Wildlife Fund (WWF) is established
	Agent orange – a chemical herbicide – is used in the Vietnam War
1962	Rachel Carson publishes *Silent Spring*

Historical timeline

1963	USA adopts the Clean Air Act
1964	USA adopts the Wilderness Act
1965	USA adopts the Land and Water Conservation Act
	Ralph Nader publishes *Unsafe at Any Speed*
1966	Kenneth E. Boulding publishes his essay 'The Economics of the Coming Spaceship Earth'
	In the USA, *The Undersea World of Jacques Cousteau* is broadcast
	The International Union for Conservation of Nature publishes its first Red Data Book on endangered species
1967	US Environmental Defense Fund is established
	Torrey Canyon oil spill occurs off the coast of Cornwall
1968	Apollo 8 mission produces first images of the Earth from space
	A biosphere conference is held in Paris
	Garrett Hardin publishes 'The Tragedy of the Commons'
	Paul Ehrlich publishes *The Population Bomb*
1969	Friends of the Earth is established
	An oil slick occurs at Santa Barbara
	Cuyahoga River fire occurs
	USA adopts the National Environmental Policy Act
1970	Natural Resources Defense Council is established
	The first Earth Day is held in the USA
	Don't Make a Wave Committee is established to protest against nuclear testing in Canada
	MIT's Study of Critical Environmental Problems publishes *Man's Impact on the Global Environment* report
	The UK Royal Commission on Environmental Pollution is established
1971	*The Founex Report* identifies the link between development and environment
	Greenpeace is established
	The US State of Oregon's Bottle Bill becomes law
	The Environmental Defense Fund wins a court order forcing the US federal government to consider a national DDT ban
	Keep America Beautiful launches the US 'Crying Indian' campaign
	Nicholas Georgescu-Roegen publishes *The Entropy Law and the Economic Process*
	Barry Commoner publishes *The Closing Circle*
	Friends of the Earth launches its first UK protest against non-returnable bottles

1972	UN Conference on the Human Environment is held in Stockholm
	The UK-based magazine *The Ecologist* publishes 'A Blueprint for Survival'
	First US Earth Day takes place on 22 April
	Club of Rome publishes *The Limits to Growth*
	James Lovelock develops his Gaia hypothesis
	Barbara Ward publishes *Only One Earth*
	USA adopts the Clean Water Act
1973	E. F. Schumacher publishes *Small is Beautiful*
	Murray Bookchin publishes *Post-Scarcity Anarchism*
	USA adopts the Endangered Species Act
	The US Ecology Center launches a recycling demonstration project in California
1974	UK adopts the Environmental Pollution Act
1975	Vietnam War ends
	RAMSAR Convention (wetlands) and CITES (wild animal trade) come into force
1976	Seveso disaster occurs in Italy, producing a dioxin cloud
	USA adopts the Resource Conservation and Recovery Act
	US Toxic Substances Control Act
1977	UK's first bottle bank is sited in Barnsley, South Yorkshire
1978	*Amoco Cadiz* oil disaster occurs near Brittany, France
	Toxic waste in the Love Canal neighbourhood in New York State is discovered
1979	Three Mile Island nuclear accident occurs in the USA
	BBC broadcasts David Attenborough's *Life on Earth* documentary
	Emergency clean-up of the Valley of the Drums – a 23-acre toxic waste dump in Kentucky
1980	The Brandt Commission publishes *North–South: A Programme for Survival*
1981	UK adopts the Wildlife and Countryside Act
	International Whaling Commission finally bans commercial whaling
	Miljöpartiet de Gröna is established as Sweden's first green political party
	Julian Simon publishes *The Ultimate Resource*
1982	Residents of Afton, a predominantly black community, protest against the construction of a hazardous waste site in North Carolina

1983	Brandt Commission publishes *Common Crisis*
	Times Beach in Missouri is evacuated due to toxin scare
1984	Union Carbide Bhopal disaster occurs in India
	Friends of the Earth launches its first UK campaign on acid rain
1985	Greenpeace's *Rainbow Warrior* is blown up by French Intelligence in Auckland, New Zealand
	Live Aid concert takes place to raise money for Ethiopian famine
1986	Chernobyl nuclear power plant explodes in Ukraine
	UK government accepts link between British air pollution and Scandinavian acid rain
	Brundtland Commission publishes *Our Common Future*
	US United Church of Christ's Commission for Racial Justice publishes *Toxic Wastes and Race*
1987	Monsanto undertakes its first GM field trials
	Economist Robert Costanza and colleagues attempt to value ecosystem services
1988	Intergovernmental Panel on Climate Change (IPCC) is established
	Miljöpartiet de Gröna is the first new political party to enter the Swedish parliament for seventy years
1989	*Exxon Valdez* oil spill occurs in Alaska
	Swedish government establishes the Stockholm Environment Institute as an international environment development research institute
	US *Time* magazine declares Endangered Earth as Planet of the Year
	UK Green Party receives 2.2 million votes in the European elections – 15 per cent of the vote
	British musician Sting establishes Rainforest Foundation International
1990	UK publishes its first environment White Paper
	IPCC publishes its first assessment report on the science of climate change
	UK adopts the Environmental Protection Act
1991	A road protest camp at Twyford Down hits the UK national news
1992	Earth Summit is held in Rio de Janeiro, Brazil
	European Union introduces a voluntary Eco-labelling scheme
	Anti-consumerist 'Buy Nothing Day' is launched in the USA

1994	US President Clinton signs an Executive Order reinforcing civil rights and environmental laws
	World Bank anniversary celebrations take place in Madrid, Spain
1995	Anti-road protests take place at Newbury bypass in Berkshire, England
	Greenpeace opposes the deep-sea disposal of Brent Spar oil storage buoy
	Finnish Greens become the first party in Western Europe to enter a national government
1996	UK Forum for the Future is established
1997	The Kyoto Protocol on climate change is adopted
1998	Veterans of the anti-roads movement and Reclaim the Streets participate in the Global Street Party to coincide with the G8 summit in Birmingham
1999	Protests take place at the Seattle World Trade Organization negotiations
2000	UK Commission on Sustainable Development is established
2001	Terrorist attacks take place on the World Trade Center in New York on 11 September
	G8 summit in Genoa (Italy) is attended by an estimated 200,000 protestors; security forces shoot dead a protestor
	IPCC publishes its third assessment report on climate change
2002	UN World Summit on Sustainable Development held in Johannesburg, South Africa
2005	Kyoto Protocol on climate change comes into force
	The UN *Millennium Ecosystem Assessment* is published
2006	US magazine *Vanity Fair* publishes a special Green Issue
	Al Gore produces the Oscar-winning climate change documentary film *An Inconvenient Truth*
	The Stern Review estimates the cost of not taking action on climate change
2007	Al Gore holds a Live Earth concert to raise awareness to combat climate change
	IPCC publishes its fourth assessment report on climate change
2008	UK adopts the world's first Climate Change Act with a legally binding commitment to reduce carbon emissions
	UNEP launches a Global Green New Deal
2009	COP 15 climate change talks held in Copenhagen (Denmark)
	Tim Jackson publishes *Prosperity Without Growth*
	University of East Anglia deals with the implications of 'climategate' email scandal

2010	US President Obama introduces the Climate Change Bill BP *Deepwater Horizon* oil spill in the Gulf of Mexico COP 16 UN climate talks take place in Cancun, Mexico Caroline Lucas is elected as Britain's first Green Party Member of Parliament
2011	UNEP publishes *Towards a Green Economy* report UK coalition government abolishes the Royal Commission on Environmental Pollution and the Commission on Sustainable Development An earthquake and tsunami threaten the operation of nuclear power plants in Japan
2012	UN Earth Summit (Rio+20) takes place in Rio de Janeiro, Brazil
2014	IPCC publishes its fifth assessment report on climate change

Acknowledgements

We would like to thank our colleagues at the Stockholm Environment Institute at the University of York for their support in writing this book. We are grateful to Professor Michael J. Chadwick, Dr John Forrester, Dr Caz Snell, Professor John Whitelegg and James Hardy for their comments and feedback on the manuscript. We thank Jennifer Allott and Andrew Greenway who read early drafts, and Erik Willis who helped in the preparation of this book. Finally, we would like to thank the staff of Routledge for their patience, and the editors of the Making of the Contemporary World Series and external reviewers for their suggestions and comments.

1 Introduction

The term 'environmentalism' encompasses a sense of concern for the environment held by hundreds of millions of people across the world. It first found popular expression during the large-scale social, economic and political changes that took place in the late 1960s. In just three years between 1969 and 1972, the campaign groups Friends of the Earth (FoE), Greenpeace and the Natural Resources Defense Council (NRDC) were founded; communities across the USA participated in the first Earth Day; governments established their first environmental agencies; and the first major United Nations Conference on the Human Environment (UNCHE) was held in Stockholm, Sweden. A *New York Times* editorial summed up the sentiment of the time: 'Call it conservation, the environment, ecological balance, or what you will, it is a cause more permanent, more far-reaching, than any issue of the era – Vietnam and Black Power included.'[1]

The environmental idea

It was only in the late nineteenth century that the word 'environment' began to take on its modern ecological meaning, to describe 'a system which includes all living things and the air, water and soil which is their habitat'.[2] Contemporary environmentalism is concerned with how society operates within this natural system. People who share this concern are called environmentalists and, in the simplest terms, believe the environment should be championed, looked after and protected. Since the end of the Second World War, this belief has become more widely held as the global speed and scale of resource use and environmental destruction have been recognised and understood. It has become more widely accepted as western standards of living have increased, basic material needs have been met, and people have demanded higher standards of environmental quality. Today, environmentalism influences the language and decisions of government, corporations and individuals to an extent that was not possible or imaginable a century ago. Politicians promise to protect the environment, companies market their products as environmentally friendly, celebrities promote environmental causes and individuals aspire to green lifestyles. The widely expressed assumption that 'green' is good can lead to the conclusion that we are all environmentalists now.

But, beyond the basic belief that the environment should be protected, there is no agreement on why this is important or how it should be done. There is no unifying set of environmental ideas to which society subscribes, nor a single environmental movement united behind a shared cause. Environmentalism has evolved in complex and sometimes contradictory ways to span conservative, reformist and radical ideas about what the world should look like, as well as how change should be brought about. These ideas are mapped and categorised by academics just as natural historians classify species of plant and animal. Recognised strands of modern environmental thinking include, but are not limited to, wilderness preservation, wildlife protection, resource conservation, human ecology, eco-feminism, eco-theology, eco-psychology, deep ecology, radical ecology, environmental justice, sustainable development and green consumerism.[3]

Each strand of modern environmental thinking brings its own set of ideas about how humanity should organise itself and interact with its environment. Over the past sixty years, these have evolved with each new environmental cause, from nuclear power and pesticide use in the 1960s to acid rain and the depletion of the ozone layer in the 1970s and 1980s and biodiversity loss and climate change in the 1990s and 2000s. Often these causes have taken hold in different countries at different times, each prompted by particular historical circumstances. For this reason, environmentalism has been taken up in many forms across generations and the continents of the world.

Scope of the book

This book examines the development of distinctive elements of contemporary environmentalism over the past sixty years. As far as possible, the early beginnings of modern environmental thought are covered, as well as the very latest ideas and events. The different philosophical perspectives of contemporary environmentalism have been covered in detail elsewhere.[4]

Each chapter of *Environmentalism since 1945* tells the story of a different aspect of environmentalism, starting with campaigns and campaign groups, then covering global environmental governance, science, economics and popular culture. Many of the oldest and most powerful campaign groups in the environmental movement were first formed or gained popular support in the USA and UK. As a consequence, many of the case studies are drawn from these two countries. Similarly, the chapter on popular culture focuses on English language references sourced predominantly from the USA and UK.

A number of themes are repeated throughout the book and are described briefly here. Firstly, the explosion of environmental activity did not represent the creation of an entirely new set of ideas. In 1885, German sociologist Max Weber (1864–1920) wrote: 'It would never occur to me to regard the enjoyment of nature as the invention of the modern age.'[5] The same can be said for modern-day interest in the environment; although the concept of the environment is relatively new, ideas and concern about humanity's relationship with nature are centuries old. Hippocrates (*ca.* 460 – *ca.* 377 BC) noted the effects of food, occupation and climate in causing disease in his book, *De aëre, aquis et locis* (*Air, Waters and Places*). The fact that modern environmental concern spread following atomic bomb tests and to the backdrop of the Vietnam War is a point much referred to by historians and environmentalists.[6] Rachel Carson's book *Silent Spring* (1962) was among the first to link the dangers of the atomic bomb to the misuse of pesticides, emphasising humanity's capacity to destroy nature and itself. Over the next ten years a number of publications followed suit: 'The Tragedy of the Commons' (Garrett Hardin, 1968) and *The Limits to Growth* (Meadows *et al.*, 1972) raised wider anxieties about the future of the planet, while 'A Blueprint for Survival' (*The Ecologist*, 1972) and *Small is Beautiful* (E. F. Schumacher, 1973) sketched out green alternatives. Almost half a century later, the anxieties expressed in each of these publications are still at the centre of many environmental concerns today.

Secondly, media coverage of dramatic pollution events has been instrumental in raising environmental concerns over the past half-century. The first major oil spill in Britain occurred when the super tanker *Torrey Canyon* struck a reef between the UK mainland and the Isles of Scilly in March 1967. The resulting oil slick covered 120 miles of Cornish coast, killing tens of thousands of birds. Two years later, an explosion on the Union Oil Company oil platform, six miles off the coast of Santa Barbara in California, resulted in the release of hundreds of thousands of gallons of crude oil. These highly visible examples of humanity's impact on the environment occurred as the age of colour television began, and broadcasters discovered that major pollution events made visually dramatic news stories. Each decade since has witnessed at least one massive oil spill from a super tanker or oil platform, serving as timely reminders that environmental issues have not gone away.

Finally, the history of contemporary environmentalism has been marked by the establishment of new institutions. Campaigns on issues such as pesticide use and nuclear testing led to the development of a new breed of professional campaign groups which have become the public face of environmentalism. At the same time, governments have responded to public concerns about the environment by establishing environmental institutions of their own. Agencies, scientific programmes, international agreements, laws and regulations have been set up to support environmental goals. All this has helped give environmentalism a permanence that has transcended the decades, much as the *New York Times* predicted.

2 The environmental movement

Over the past fifty years there has been an unprecedented growth in public concern for the environment.[1] The 1960s saw a surge in environmental activity driven by transformative social, cultural and political events. This resulted in the emergence of a new social movement that furthered the environmental agenda by mobilising public opinion and forcing governments and businesses to take action. The new breed of international environmental campaign groups founded at this time took on a set of environmental issues that went beyond the narrower wildlife and wilderness protection interests of earlier groups. The moral entrepreneurship of this new generation of campaign groups increased public awareness of environmental issues and helped to define and shape a wide range of environmental debates.[2] As campaigning groups professionalised their operations and took on a more corporate character, the 1980s and 1990s saw the formation of distinct, community-based offshoots of the environmental movement, in part as a response to globalisation. By the turn of the twenty-first century, the environmental movement had become as diverse and complex as the environmental issues it faced. It continues to evolve and has adapted to address new environmental challenges, developing new campaign tactics to achieve its goals.

Early environmental campaigns

Environmental campaigning can be traced back to the late nineteenth century, when Europe and North America experienced a growth in social movements.[3] Early environmental campaigners were concerned about rapidly industrialising and expanding cities encroaching fields, forests and wilderness areas. Groups were formed to protect landscapes for their aesthetic and recreational value and to preserve access to, and enjoyment of, scenic landscapes as a 'national property, in which every man has a right and interest who has an eye to perceive and a heart to enjoy'.[4]

An early battleground for US and UK environmental campaigners was the damming of valleys to supply water and energy to nearby cities. Campaigners relied on establishing relationships with powerful figures who could influence legislation or donate money. Campaigns were volunteer-led, and were generally supported by rich members of society.[5] Some of today's best known environmental organisations were established to campaign to protect places of natural beauty. In the UK, the National Trust (est. 1895) purchased many of its early properties and land in the Lake District shortly after Thirlmere reservoir was built to supply water to Manchester.[6] In the USA, the Sierra Club (est. 1892) waged a long campaign against the city of San Francisco to stop a dam being built in the Hetch Hetchy Valley in Yosemite National Park. With just 1000 members across the USA, the Sierra Club could not rely on the spectacle of marches or loud protests. Instead, alternative campaign tactics were employed, including letter writing and distribution of pamphlets to members of Congress. The pamphlets promoted the romance and beauty of Yosemite, and contained photos and writing by John Muir (1838–1914), founder of the Sierra Club.[7]

Many early environmental groups followed the National Trust's approach to achieving protected designation for specific areas. In the UK, the Society for the Promotion of Nature Reserves (est. 1912), later to become the Wildlife Trust, compiled a list of areas that deserved protection and raised money to purchase land. The Royal Society for the Protection of Birds (RSPB) (est. 1889) did not purchase its first nature reserves until 1930, but by 1941 it was managing fifteen reserves.[8] In the 1930s and 1940s, the Council for the Preservation of Rural England (CPRE) (est. 1926; now the Campaign to Protect Rural England) focused on the planning system and secured early restrictions to town and country development through Acts of Parliament.

In the USA, outdoors, hunting, fishing and wildlife enthusiasts began to conserve and protect birds, mammals and wilderness areas. The National Audubon Society (est. 1905) took its name from John James Audubon, the author of *Birds of America* (1840). The Society's first campaigns were against hunting for bird plumage, mirroring campaigns in the UK against plumes for women's hats, led by the RSPB.

Other environmental organisations active today, but established in the first half of the twentieth century, include the Izaak Walton League (est. 1922), the Wilderness Society (est. 1935), National Wildlife Federation (est. 1936), and Defenders of Wildlife (est. 1947). But during this time, membership of many of these environmental organisations remained low. By 1950 the Sierra Club's membership had grown to just 7000, and by 1960 the RSPB reached 10,000 members for the very first time.[9,10] Few environmental organisations had paid staff, as funding was directed to land purchase or campaigning activities. However, membership of these organisations rose rapidly following an increase in public awareness and concern. Social, economic and political changes in wider society, rather than specific campaign activities, drove this public engagement with environmental issues. As new environmental issues came to the fore, a wave of campaigns and groups emerged to tackle them, creating a new and distinctive social movement.

Dawn of a new movement

The 1960s saw the construction of a concrete wall separating East Berlin from West Berlin, decolonisation of former British colonies, selection of John F. Kennedy as the thirty-fifth US President, the assassination of Martin Luther King, and increasing anti-communist feeling in the West. In the USA, growing opposition to the nuclear bomb, the Vietnam War and the use of chemical herbicide defoliants known as Agent Orange coincided with the emergence of a counter-culture and an increasingly widespread tendency to question established values and institutions. This was driven by a new generation of young people who were openly critical and rebellious. It was also a time when opposition against the state and industrial society became a unifying force for students across Europe and North America. In France, the New Left attempted to overthrow the government, while the American Students for a Democratic Society recruited members across university campuses. Hundreds of thousands of people were mobilised to march for civil rights and against the Vietnam War. This rebellious period in history provided the backdrop for the birth of the modern environmental movement. Individuals made links between social and environmental concerns, such as war, nuclear testing and chemical pesticides. Campaigns were launched, and small, effective campaign groups were founded and quickly gained momentum.

Over a ten-year period (1961–71), many major environmental organisations were established. These included the World Wildlife Fund in Switzerland (WWF) (est. 1961; now the World Wide Fund for Nature)[11;] and in North America, the Environmental Defense Fund (EDF) (est. 1967), FoE (est. 1969), NRDC (est. 1970) and Greenpeace (est. 1971). In Europe, new green political parties were formed that contested elections but also acted as campaign groups. This loosely connected movement represented a large, young, educated and idealistic constituency, equally concerned about issues of peace, civil rights and global environmental destruction. The following three sections outline the early development of the movement in the USA and Europe, and on the global stage.

US environmental successes

Throughout the 1960s and 1970s, US environmental groups, campaigning for stricter national pollution control laws as well as agencies with the power to enforce them, helped to achieve a number of legislative milestones. These included the National Environmental Policy Act, Clean Air Act, Clean Water Act and Endangered Species Act. A characteristic of this rapidly expanding movement was new and old campaign groups working together. Scientists and legal experts either founded, or were employed by, new groups, and filed environmental lawsuits that delayed or halted government and industrial activities. A 1971 Associated Press article published as 'Revolt of the Bird Watchers' documents a lawsuit by FoE and the EDF stalling construction of a US$2.5 billion Alaskan oil pipeline. Another, from the National Wildlife Federation and the Sierra Club, forced the Atomic Energy Commission to re-examine the environmental impact of an atomic energy plant in Calvert Cliffs, Maryland.[12]

The EDF's campaigns to ban the pesticide dichlorodiphenyltrichloroethane (DDT) have become an iconic legal battle. After the Second World War, DDT's insecticidal properties were hailed for their contribution to disease prevention. However, some scientists and federal agencies wanted to restrict its application. Over the next decade, public concern increased, with articles in *Reader's Digest*, *Life* and *Sports Illustrated* raising public fears about the effects of aerial spraying of DDT. In 1962, Rachel Carson brought DDT aerial spraying to widespread public attention through her bestselling book *Silent Spring* (see Chapter 4).[13] The US government's failure to respond to these concerns provided the opportunity for citizens' law suits against the use of DDT. In 1971 the EDF, with support from the Izaak Walton League and National Audubon Society, won a court order forcing the federal government to consider a national DDT ban, which Congress adopted a year later. Over the next forty years, law suits and legislative battles were to become a key feature of the US environmental movement.

European mobilisation

During this period, US environmental groups quickly established a presence in Europe. In 1971, FoE took its first steps towards becoming an international network with a meeting of representatives from France, Sweden, UK and the USA. From the beginning, FoE UK focused on influencing national policy through a combination of professional advocacy and local group action. Local groups could choose the national campaigns they wanted to support which addressed a number of international and domestic campaign priorities.

In 1971, FoE UK launched its first campaign against non-returnable bottles, linked to a wider message about the wastefulness of a throwaway society.[14] This began with the type of publicity stunt that has become a common feature of the environmental movement. Hundreds of glass bottles were dumped outside the front door of the London headquarters of Schweppes. The stunt secured headlines across the national press and helped FoE create a national profile. Local groups were soon established across the country, lending support to the actions of the central office through letter-writing campaigns, petitions and local meetings.

During the 1970s and 1980s, European campaign groups began to establish themselves as a counter power to the main political parties. Tom Burke, Director of FoE UK (1975–79), described himself as an 'environmental politician'.[15] Meanwhile, FoE UK's sister group in France, *Les Amis del la Terre*, fielded Brice Lalonde (b. 1946) as a candidate for the *Mouvement d'Ecologie Politique* in the 1981 Presidential elections and won 3.9 per cent of the total vote. Green politics was becoming more explicit as campaigners linked social and environmental agendas to create new political parties across Europe.

Sweden's *Miljöpartiet de gröna* was among the first green parties to secure national electoral success in Europe. Founded in 1981, it took less than a decade to establish itself on the national scene. By 1988, environmental issues were at the top of the political agenda and dominated the election campaign. *Miljöpartiet* received 5.5 per cent of the vote and gained twenty seats in parliament, making it the first new party to enter parliament for seventy years.[16,17] Elsewhere in Europe, the Finnish Green League (*Vihreä liitto*) secured parliamentary recognition in 1991, and became the first green party in Western Europe to enter a national government in 1995. In Central and Eastern Europe during the 1990s, communist-ruled countries such as the Czech Republic, Hungary and Poland also saw the development of environmental movements. The size, organisation and independence of groups in each of these countries reflected their particular national political and environmental challenges. During the Soviet leadership of Mikhail Gorbachev (b. 1931) (1988–91), environmental activism in communist countries was seen as a safe way of criticising the Soviet regime, and environmental groups mobilised a great deal of public support. During the transition from communist rule, environmental issues dropped down the political agenda as the focus of citizens turned to institutional change and political and economic reform.

The most successful European environment-focused political party is *Bündnis 90/Die Grünen*, which grew out of a partnership of the West German Green Party (est. 1979) and an East German alliance of parties in 1993. Post-war transformation and an acute generation gap have been seen as providing the social base for the rise of the German Greens, while frustrations over policy and opposition to nuclear power provided the impetus for the formation of a political party.[18] Like many green parties in Europe, the West German Green Party had its roots in the student protests of the late 1960s. Petra Kelly (1947–92), one of its founders, was involved in political campaigning in the USA. Daniel Cohn-Bendit (b. 1945), now a leading green campaigner in France and Germany, was a student leader involved in the 1968 attempt to overthrow the French government. He, along with Joschka Fischer (b. 1948), a future Foreign Minister and Vice Chancellor of Germany, were associated with a number of radical and revolutionary groups in the 1960s and 1970s.

Green political parties established themselves throughout Europe and most western economies because existing parties were not able to address the environmental agenda adequately. The fledgling German political movement set the tone with the slogan 'we are neither left or right: we are in front'. Although no two green parties were exactly alike, most were committed to grassroots democracy, non-violence and social justice. As one of the first parties to win electoral seats at regional and state level, the German Greens used their platform to challenge traditional models of economic growth, called for a reduced-hour working week, and demanded an end to nuclear power.[19]

In 1980s West Germany, the anti-nuclear movement was almost identical to the environmental movement, and the Green Party acted as its parliamentary arm. In the UK, the link between early forms of the Green Party and campaign groups were less established, and environmental campaign groups continued to make the greater impact. FoE led a campaign against the reprocessing of spent nuclear fuels, claiming it would turn the UK into a nuclear dustbin for the world. A coalition of groups campaigned effectively to force a review of the UK fast breeder nuclear reactor programme. During this period the People Party, which changed its name to the Ecology Party in 1975 and later to the Green Party of England and Wales in 1990, held explicit anti-nuclear stances but had little electoral impact.

European opposition to nuclear energy reached its height after the 1986 Chernobyl nuclear disaster. To mark the first anniversary of the disaster, FoE and the Campaign for Nuclear Disarmament (CND) organised a protest in the UK attended by 100,000 people. By 1989, a decline in the popularity of the UK Conservative government, driven by growing opposition to the Community Charge, also known as the Poll Tax, was combined with public concern over nuclear power and the depletion of the ozone layer. Sara Parkin (b. 1946), co-secretary and spokesperson for the UK Green Party, was able to mobilise this discontent.[20] In the 1989 European Parliamentary Elections, the UK Green Party won the support of 2.2 million people – equivalent to 15 per cent of the vote. Despite this success, it failed to gain any seats in the following general election. This has been attributed to a number of causes, including the British first-past-the post electoral system, and resistance within the Green Party to reforms intended to make it more electable. Over the next two decades internal reforms were slowly put into place, but it took until 2010 for Caroline Lucas (b. 1960) to be elected as Britain's first Green Party Member of Parliament, for Brighton Pavilion. Today, European green parties collaborate in national government coalitions and have a strong presence in the European Parliament.

Global environmental campaigns

By the 1970s, a new breed of environmental organisation had emerged that led high-profile environmental campaigns aimed at a global impact. This reflected an understanding of transboundary pollution, and a growing recognition of habitat destruction and the threat it posed to wildlife. Greenpeace, FoE and WWF were at the forefront of many of these campaigns, aimed at influencing national governments and global institutions such as the UN.

In 1960, British biologist Sir Julian Huxley (1887–1975), first Director General of the UN Educational, Scientific and Cultural Organization (UNESCO), undertook a wildlife conservation trip to East Africa. On his return he wrote three articles for the UK's *Observer* newspaper warning the British public that the rate of habitat destruction and hunting of Africa's wildlife could mean extinction over the next two decades. Responding to this, Max Nicholson (1904–2003), Director General of Britain's Nature Conservancy, gathered together a group of scientists and advertising and public relations experts, all committed to establishing an international organisation that became known as WWF.[21] What made WWF a thoroughly modern campaign group was its focus on the need to raise funds for environmental action, and as a consequence it developed new fundraising strategies. In 1961, WWF launched its first British fundraising appeal with a special issue of the *Daily Mirror* newspaper. Pictures of black rhinos featured on the front page of the tabloid with the headline 'Doomed', together with WWF's panda logo – perhaps the most widely recognised environmental logo in the world today. As a tabloid newspaper, the *Daily Mirror* audience reached far beyond the young radicals of the 1960s and the educated middle classes. By using mainly emotional appeals focusing on attractive animals, WWF found a way of engaging a broad section of the public and succeeded in raising large sums of money. In its first three years, US$1.9 million was donated to projects across Africa, Europe and India.[22]

Greenpeace engaged global audiences in a very different way. It can trace its beginnings to a group of peace activists who wanted to stop US nuclear bomb testing at Amchitka Island off the west coast of Alaska. The group called themselves the Don't Make a Wave Committee (est. 1970), and decided the best way they could stop the nuclear tests was to charter a ship to sail from Vancouver into the test zone. The activists called the ship *Greenpeace*, to capture what they considered 'the two great issues of the time – survival of our environment and peace of the world'.[23] Greenpeace's first voyage failed to stop the Amchitka test, but gained national media coverage. Nuclear testing on Amchitka ended that same year, and the island was later declared a bird sanctuary. Taking the name of the ship as an inspiration, key members of the Don't Make a Wave Committee established Greenpeace (est. 1971) as a campaign organisation. The Quaker philosophy of bearing witness, demonstrating passive resistance by placing campaigners at the scene of environmental problems has been fundamental to Greenpeace campaigns ever since.

Since the 1970s, Save the Whale has been a signature campaign for many groups. Greenpeace campaigners secured widespread news coverage when they used high-speed inflatable boats to block whaling ship operations. The risk associated with these actions demonstrated how serious Greenpeace activists considered the environmental threat to be, and was intended to overturn any view of whaling as a heroic or brave activity.[24] This approach succeeded in getting the US public and politicians in particular to put pressure on whaling nations to stop hunting activities. Following lobbying by the US government among others, the International Whaling Commission finally took the decision to ban commercial whaling in 1982, with the ban coming into force in 1986.

Governments did not always tolerate Greenpeace's direct action approach, especially with regard to the issues of whaling and nuclear tests. In 1985, a diver attached a limpet mine to the Greenpeace boat *Rainbow Warrior* while it was docked in Auckland, New Zealand. The mine exploded, causing a hole in the side of the boat, and killed one of the ship's crew. Later it emerged that the mine had been planted by the French Intelligence Agency to prevent Greenpeace from protesting against French nuclear testing in Moruroa Atoll. This action alone, and its tragic consequences, demonstrated the extent to which the French government perceived Greenpeace campaigns as damaging to national interests.

By now, predominantly UK- and US-based environmental campaign groups had established global audiences, and many of them expanded and affiliated to other groups across the world. In 1986 FoE International had a confederation of thirty-one member groups, many of which existed and campaigned in their own right before becoming affiliated to the global network. By 2010, the network was made up of seventy-seven members and affiliated groups, with a high number in developing countries. The make-up of FoE international membership meant that it was among the first environmental pressure groups to launch international campaigns on developing world issues such as the protection of tropical forests. This, combined with its explicit recognition of human rights and development needs, has made it a natural ally of human rights and international development groups.

A new wave of grassroots movements

The 1980s and 1990s saw the emergence of a new wave of high-profile grassroots and community-based movements. The US environmental justice and the UK anti-roads movements emerged in response to planning decisions that appeared to give priority to private or government interests over community interests. These movements focused on environmental issues, but were distinct from established environmental groups and green political parties. Many of the participants in the US environmental justice movement were African or Latin American and had strong links to the civil rights campaigns, church-based activism and workplace struggles of the 1960s.[25] The UK anti-roads movement had strong countercultural roots and drew on a long tradition of direct action in the country. Many participants were influenced by tactics used by Greenpeace, Earth First! and the peace movement, including the women's peace camps at the Royal Air Force Base at Greenham Common.[26]

Both the US environmental justice movement and the UK anti-roads movement shared a lack of confidence in established environmental groups to address the issues that were important to them. This led to new and distinctive coalitions and campaign tactics that contributed to the development of the 1990s global countercultural movement. During this time, concerns over social, economic and environmental justice began to centre on global economic and trade agreements. The campaigns that followed brought together a wide range of established and grassroots groups from the environmental movement and beyond.

The environmental justice movement emerged against a backdrop of wider public concern over environmental pollution in the USA, but was framed by the issue of racial discrimination. From the late 1970s onwards, a number of highly publicised pollution incidents raised public fears of toxic pollution. These included the 1978 discovery of toxic waste in the Love Canal neighbourhood in New York State, and the 1983 permanent evacuation of Times Beach in Missouri due to a toxin scare. Vivid images of the problem were provided by media coverage of the 1979 emergency clean up of the Valley of the Drums – a twenty-three-acre toxic waste dump in Kentucky. The beginning of the movement is widely associated with a 1982 protest against a newly constructed hazardous waste landfill site by residents of Afton, a predominantly black community in Warren County in North Carolina. After failing to halt the construction of the site, a number of local residents resorted to lying down in front of trucks to stop them from entering the site. Six weeks of marches and protests followed and more than 500 people were arrested.

The US authorities had attempted to respond to the issue of abandoned hazardous waste sites through measures such as the 1980 Superfund set up to fund site clean ups. However, concern at the siting of toxic waste dumps in poor or black communities continued. In 1987, the United Church of Christ's Commission for Racial Justice published *Toxic Wastes and Race*.[27] The study found that race was the strongest variable in predicting the siting of waste facilities. This galvanised the movement nationally to oppose environmental racism. In 1994, President Bill Clinton recognised the importance of this issue when he signed an Executive Order reinforcing civil rights and environmental laws and requiring federal regulatory agencies to consider environmental justice in all their work.

Nowadays the US environment justice movement has moved beyond an anti-toxics focus to include wider issues, including public health, transport and land use. National networks are now established that bring together an alliance of community activists, lawyers, academics and concerned citizens. The major environmental campaign groups are still largely uninvolved, but the movement has demonstrated a longevity and impact without them.[28] Outside the USA, environmental justice has become an increasingly important theme in many parts of the world. The relationship between income (rather than race) and pollution exposure is a real issue in many countries, as is the ability of local communities to access benefits from the exploitation of globally important resources. International campaign groups such as FoE are active on these issues. So too are specialist groups such as Global Witness (est. 1993), which tackles the links between trade in natural resources, human rights abuses, corruption and conflict.

The UK anti-roads movement is an example of a single-issue campaign that was supported by a wide range of groups from inside and outside the environmental movement. It emerged in the early 1990s with renewed public interest in the environment. In the same year that the UK Green Party had achieved success in the 1989 European elections, the Conservative Prime Minister Margaret Thatcher gave a speech on climate change at the UN. A year later, the British Government published *This Common Inheritance* (1990), the first ever White Paper on the environment.[29] A less welcome development for environmentalists was the Conservative government's plans for the 'largest road-building programme in the UK since the Romans', set out in the 1989 transport White Paper *Roads for Prosperity* (1989).

FoE had campaigned against road schemes since 1972, and in 1976 published *Getting Nowhere Fast*, questioning the desirability of increased car use. Other groups, including CPRE, formed the Transport Reform Group and lobbied against further road building, but the Conservative government was not proving responsive. A number of public enquiries into road-building developments had been subject to direct action interventions by a combination of local community groups and anti-road activists. As new road schemes reached the implementation stage, this civil disobedience moved from courtrooms to the planned road routes. Twyford Down was the first road protest camp to hit the national news in 1991. The protest lasted one year and was followed by mass trespass events along the motorway. Other road protests included those on the M17 through Glasgow from 1993 to

1995 ('the Pollock Free State'), and the M11 link road in London and the Newbury bypass in 1995.

In most cases, the road protests were a final, desperate act after all other strategies had failed. The campaign for Twyford Down had lasted almost twenty years. During this campaign, FoE, Greenpeace and other environmental groups took the Department for Transport to the UK High Court, but lost. In only a few cases did these road protests succeed in stopping the building of the roads in question. What they did achieve was to slow down and increase the cost of the national road-building process. The Conservative government's road-building programme was scaled down over time and eventually cancelled in 1997 by the incoming Labour Government.

A feature of many of the UK road protests was an alliance between local residents, established environmental groups and more radical environmental campaigners. Newly established non-violent direct action groups such as Earth First! (a US import) and Reclaim the Streets organised, or were present at, many road protest camps. By occupying and locking themselves to trees, digging tunnels and doing everything they could to disrupt road-building operations, they developed a new public image of the modern environmentalist. They also showed that campaign groups with limited resources and few links to the political establishment could use direct action to damage the reputation and increase the financial costs of large-scale infrastructure programmes over time.

A global counterculture

In the 1990s, environmental issues once again become widely incorporated in a growing anti-establishment movement that was distrustful of global brands and multinational corporations. The anti-consumerist Buy Nothing Day, first launched in the USA in 1992, encapsulated the ideals of this countercultural movement. It became increasingly visible as a protest movement on city streets following trade negotiations and economic summits across the world. Early large-scale street protests began with the '50 Years is Enough' campaign. This campaign brought together campaigners from trade justice, development and environment communities to protest against the policies of the International Monetary Fund (IMF), World Bank and World Trade Organization (WTO). During the 1994 World Bank anniversary celebrations in Madrid, Spain, Greenpeace activists interrupted proceedings, showering attendees with fake dollar bills while protesters chanted outside.[30] Meetings of the G8[31] also became targets of international protests. In 1998, veterans of the anti-roads movement and Reclaim the Streets participated in the Global Street Party that coincided with the twenty-fourth G8 summit in Birmingham in the UK.

A global network of individuals and organisations grew out of this series of coordinated protests. It was supported by increased use of the internet and do-it-yourself media to share videos, news and articles on protests across the world. When activists established an independent media centre for anyone to upload news and reports from the 1989 WTO Seattle protests, the website received over a million hits over a couple of days.[32]

Environmental issues were a key concern of activists protesting outside the Seattle WTO negotiations in 1999. The environment was also a stumbling block for nations that struggled to agree on whether environmental standards equated to trade protectionism. As citizens from across the world filled the streets, the established environmental groups briefed the world's media that deals behind closed doors could endanger global development and the environment. It was common for both environment and development movements to work together at these international WTO gatherings.

The anti-globalisation protests of the late 1990s had distinctive organisational features. They were loosely coordinated, involved a broad range of participants, and linked together a wide range of social, economic and environmental issues. They also brought considerable security concerns to cities hosting heads of state from many countries. As a result, the police response to protests was often draconian and confrontations with protestors could be violent. This came to a head at the 2001 G8 summit in Genoa, Italy attended by an estimated 200,000 protestors. Over two days of running battles between protestors and security forces, a man was shot dead and organisers of the local independent media centre were badly beaten by Italian police.[33]

The Genoa protests occurred months before the 9/11 terrorists attacks on the World Trade Center in New York, and thereafter the oppositional spectacle of anti-globalisation protests declined sharply as governments introduced stricter security at international talks. Those willing to protest had to travel to isolated venues and rarely got close to delegates. By 2003, large-scale anti-globalisation protests had given way to anti-war protests in the run up to the war in Iraq.

Away from the media headlines of large-scale protest, it is clear that the anti-globalisation movement helped bring together a loose global network of civil society organisations, including those addressing environmental matters. These networks continue to develop through a number of avenues such as the World Social Forum, which has met on a regular basis since 2001.

Contemporary campaign challenges

There has been continuous growth in the number of environmental campaigns, groups and members in both the UK and USA. Today, membership of the largest US environmental organisations is estimated to stand at approximately 10 million – a hundredfold growth since 1950s. Estimates of the UK's ten largest environmental campaign groups suggest a collective membership of 5 million people.[34] On a global level, hundreds of millions of people engage in collective activity on behalf of the environment. Many of these people will participate in a single action or event, sign a petition against a company practice, or campaign against environmental damage in their area. Often they will identify their action with a wider environmental cause and sometimes with a wider environmental movement. This is both a weakness and strength of the modern environmental movement. The movement has tended to consist of a loosely connected set of campaigns and actions that are rarely brought together on a global scale.

The professional campaign groups that are closely associated with the environmental movement provide some coordination, but also compete for attention, funding and support. There is high public awareness of environmental issues, but less mass commitment to taking action and sustained campaigning. Every new environmental campaign enters a crowded market place, where messaging, branding and impact are sometimes as important as the environmental goal. At the same time, new global and highly complex issues have emerged while many 'old' environmental issues remain unresolved. Habitat destruction and major pollution incidents continue while the threat of climate change poses further global challenges. At the international level, global institutions and nation states struggle to reach agreement on how to address these challenges. In the face of this, the environmental movement has disagreed over what the world should look like and how to get there, and has limited success in securing an appropriate policy response.

A crowded marketplace

As environmental campaign groups have developed, it has become clear that they have distinct differences in approach to achieving environmental goals. These differences can be seen in the way groups have directed and funded their campaigns: for some, a large membership base is as important as it was in the 1960s; for others, corporate and governmental partnerships are an increasingly important focus.

Greenpeace is a highly centralised organisation, but has always relied on individual members and supporters to fund its campaigns and maintain its independence. Greenpeace International has approximately 3 million members, giving it the financial independence to be able to campaign against high-profile global corporations. Over the past twenty years, it has launched campaigns that have brought about concessions or changes in corporate policy[35] by Apple, Bayer,[36] Coca Cola,[37] Dell,[38] McDonalds,[39] Monsanto[40] and Nestlé,[41] among many others.

Whereas most Greenpeace actions over the past forty years have been undertaken by a handful of committed activists, it now mobilises internet activists across the globe to support its campaigns. Internet activism can be undertaken from the comfort of home, and is cheap, easy and effective. In 2006, Greenpeace launched the Green My Apple campaign when it found Apple less responsive than other computer companies to removing hazardous substances from products. Targeting Apple's brand strength and consumer status, Greenpeace created a website aimed at Apple fans.[42] Through the website, Greenpeace made it clear that it wanted Apple fans to run the campaign and create campaign material. It provided online images and design material for visitors to create and post imaginative ways of pushing the campaign using their Apple Macintosh computers.[43] The response from Apple users was rapid, and within months the company had responded, committing among other things to phasing out what Greenpeace considered the worst chemicals in the Apple product range.

The scope for targeted internet activism and the demonstration of support it provides means that many campaign groups make a point of highlighting this strength. FoE International claims over 2 million members and supporters, and the NRDC illustrates its strength by referring to its 1.3 million members and online activists. Although the campaign groups established in the 1960s and 1970s saw rapid increases in membership, it is the older, established nature conservation groups that have the highest membership and income levels. In the UK, the National Trust is the largest environmental group, followed by the RSPB. In the USA, the National Wildlife Federation has one of the largest memberships. Part of the reason for these higher membership numbers is that many of these groups offer access to nature reserves and historic landscapes in return for membership. Supporters of these groups appreciate and care for the environment, but they are not signing up to an activist package. Occasionally, RSPB and the National Trust will join with other campaign organisations in a show of strength that demonstrates the size of the environmental constituency. At other times, they leave campaigning to activist groups.

Over the past thirty years, some environmental groups have shifted their focus from recruiting members of the public to establishing partnerships with governments and corporations. The US-based group Conservation International (est. 1987) partnered with other organisations from the beginning, reasoning that no organisation can get the job done alone. It has worked with Starbucks and Walmart, among others, to 'make conservation part of their business model'.[44] Groups tackling a wide range of environmental issues now take this approach and are not supported by individual members. Forum for the Future (est. 1996) promotes its work on sustainable development through partnerships with organisations such as BT, Tesco and Unilever.

WWF has managed to sustain large membership levels and to work in partnership with a wide range of companies. In 2002, WWF International, together with Earthwatch and Botanic Gardens Conservation International, joined the HSBC bank in a five-year, £35 million partnership. Consistent with WWF's objectives, this secured the charity £12.7 million for conservation projects along the Yangtze, Rio Grande and Amazon rivers.[45] This level of investment is difficult to secure from membership alone, and provides organisations such as WWF the means to meet specific objectives in target areas.

Critics of such partnerships argue that they do not improve the environmental performance of partners, but serve to justify wider patterns of environmental destruction.[46] Nor do they necessarily provide companies with protection from the criticism of other environmental campaigns. Two years after the WWF deal, FoE accused HSBC of financing forest destruction and social conflict, and stated that over the previous ten years it had helped arrange over US$1.6 billion in loans and credit guarantees to the palm oil sector in Indonesia.[47]

Sometimes differences in approach result in environmental campaign groups publicly disagreeing. In 2009, Greenpeace published the findings of its investigation of the Noel Kampff Climate Action Project, a protected forest area set up in 1997 by the Nature Conservancy, BP, Pacificorp, American Electric Power and the Bolivian Government. It described the project as a 'carbon scam', contradicted claims that it produced scientifically quantifiable carbon emissions reductions, and called into question whether it had provided sustainable benefits and alternative livelihoods to local communities.[48] The Nature Conservancy brushed these criticisms aside, and stated that the Noel Kempff project:

> serves as an example of how well-designed forest carbon projects can result in real, scientifically measurable and verifiable emissions

reductions with important benefits for biodiversity and local communities.[49]

Disagreements of this kind, questions of transparency and trust, and concerns that green groups have become 'just another special interest' provide the contemporary environmental movement with new challenges. In several countries, and in the USA in particular, counter-movements have been established to oppose environmental causes. The counter-movement has taken many forms, including the Wise Use Movement and the Global Climate Coalition (see Chapters 4 and 7); often these are industry-led and have received popular support. Taken together, the establishment of an organised opposition, as well as problems within the environmental movement, have come to the fore at a time when the attention of the entire movement has turned to one topic – climate change.

Tackling climate change

Every environmental campaign group, regardless of its founding objectives and purpose, has a stance on climate change. The issue has the potential to unify the environmental movement as well as to be a cause of great disagreement. In the UK, innovative partnerships and new forms of movement organisation have characterised climate change campaigns. These have influenced, supported and strengthened UK government action on climate change. In particular, the FoE's The Big Ask campaign helped create the public momentum needed for the UK government to adopt the 2008 Climate Change Act, which set the world's first legally binding targets to reduce six greenhouse gases by 80 per cent by 2050 compared with a 1990 baseline. The Act aims to enable the UK to make the transition to a low-carbon economy, and resulted in the independent Committee on Climate Change being established to provide advice to government on these targets and related policies.

Thom Yorke (b. 1968), lead singer of the music group Radiohead, launched The Big Ask campaign on 25 May 2005. The launch coincided with a national opinion poll survey showing that 73 per cent of the UK public thought the government was not doing enough to tackle climate change. On the same day, a Parliamentary petition (Early Day Motion 178) opened calling for new legislation requiring annual cuts in carbon dioxide emissions of 3 per cent. In September 2006, the campaign group made an extra effort to encourage MPs to sign the

Early Day Motion and to write to the Prime Minister calling for a new climate law. Over the following weeks, FoE mobilised the public to personally lobby 620 out of a total of 646 MPs to back its campaign. FoE also joined a climate change coalition of mainly environmental and international development NGOs. The Stop Climate Chaos coalition ran the I Count campaign and organised a climate change rally in London to urge the government to introduce a climate change bill.

On 26 October 2008, the climate law became a reality, and the first law of its kind in the world. Inspired by the UK success, a European campaign was launched in 2009 with similar laws being submitted to parliament in Austria, Belgium, Finland, Malta, Ireland and Scotland. A total of eighteen European countries became part of The Big Ask campaign, demanding strong and fair climate laws which will introduce binding annual cuts in greenhouse gas emissions.[50]

The UK environmental movement also had success in challenging government decisions that did not appear to support the new Climate Change Bill. Over a number of years, a wide coalition of campaign groups, including Campaign for Better Transport, Climate Camp, FoE, National Trust, Greenpeace, Society for the Protection of Ancient Buildings, and Plane Stupid, worked together to make the proposal for a third runway at London Heathrow airport politically unpalatable. Direct action, a high-profile Heathrow land purchase by Greenpeace, and opposition from the National Trust and RSPB combined to provide opposition to the airport expansion. On 26 March 2010, a High Court judge ruled that the government's policy for the expansion of Heathrow airport, first set out in 2003, would need to be re-examined. In May 2010, the newly elected Conservative and Liberal Democrat coalition government cancelled plans for the third runway at Heathrow and ruled out new runways at Stansted and Gatwick airports. This compares with the unsuccessful campaign Coalition Against Runway 2 (CAR2) to stop the construction of a second runway at Manchester's International Airport in 1997.

In the USA, the environmental movement has been less effective in addressing climate change compared with issues associated with clean air, water, wilderness and wildlife. Over the past twenty years, green campaigns have been launched in support of a series of legislative climate change bills, and at the time of writing each one has failed. In some cases effective campaigning has been held back by disagreement over aims and tactics between larger 'establishment' groups and smaller, more radical groups. In May 2010, the Obama Administration introduced a long-awaited Climate Change Bill, the American Power Act, which sought to reduce carbon emissions by 17 per cent by 2020 compared with 2005 levels. This initial target is modest compared with the European Union (EU). However, further cuts would eliminate 42 per cent of emissions by 2030 and 83 per cent by 2050 compared with 2005 levels. The Bill is based on a 'cap-and-trade' system – a market-based mechanism that sets a cap on overall emissions and then requires companies in the energy and transport sectors to obtain emission allowances to emit greenhouse gases.[51] In July 2010, the US Senate announced that it was postponing the advancement of the Climate Change Bill due to wide opposition among Republican lawmakers and some Democrats. The postponement was considered to be caused by a number of factors, including the partisan battle over healthcare reform, the *Deepwater Horizon* oil spill in the Gulf of Mexico, and the expectation that the Democrats would lose seats in the November 2010 elections.[52] However, the decision to strike the bill from the Senate's immediate agenda was seen as yet another failure by the US environmental movement to secure the public momentum needed to secure a Climate Change Bill.

Whereas the tactics of established campaign groups have been challenged, a new breed of civil society organisations are widely seen as being at the forefront of efforts to organise action against climate change. In the UK, the Transition Towns movement has provided a community-led response to climate change and peak oil. There are over 250 transition towns and cities, spanning twelve countries, working to raise awareness of green living.[53] In the USA, the Interfaith Power and Light network has provided a religious response to climate change. The progressive MoveOn network has approximately 3 million members across the USA, and since 2003 has consistently made energy and environmental issues a campaign priority. New internet-based campaign groups have demonstrated the scope for a single global campaign for action on climate change. Avaaz, a web-based campaign community, uses the model pioneered by MoveOn. It claims 3.3 million members across 192 countries, and campaigns on a wide range of social, economic and environmental issues, including climate change. In 2009, the campaign group 350 organised the single largest international campaign on climate change. The campaign focused on achieving 350 parts per million of carbon dioxide, as levels above this figure would accelerate climate change. Through the internet and other media channels, the 350 campaign organised a global day of action. A total of 5200 demonstrations took place in 181 countries, involving groups from across the environmental spectrum and beyond it to religious, sporting and cultural spheres.

Understanding the environmental movement

This chapter has examined the emergence of contemporary environmentalism as a new social movement from its early beginnings in nature conservation to the rise of a global anti-consumerism counterculture. Before the Second World War, environmentalism was a minority concern, supported by those wealthy enough to look beyond immediate material needs. The post-war improvements in living standards, together with increased awareness of environmental pollution and changes in culture, have made the wider public more receptive to calls for action on environmental issues. The first generation of post-war environmental campaigners used a combination of science, powerful imagery and new campaign tactics to bring about changes in public attitudes, commercial behaviour and government policy. The campaign groups that people most readily link to environmentalism were formed at this time, attracted large memberships, and became increasingly professional and institutionalised in character.

The ability of the environmental movement to bring about change through targeted campaigns has been both a great strength and a weakness. Campaign slogans such as 'stop whaling', 'save the rainforest' and 'ban unleaded petrol', together with stunts, public demonstrations and celebrity endorsements, have all assisted in capturing the attention of the media, raising public awareness and subsequently action. Nevertheless, public attention has rarely remained focused on any particular issue for very long. The rise and fall of public interest in environmental issues has been described as an 'issue–attention cycle'.[54] Typically, environmental problems come to prominence due to scientific discovery, and campaign groups demand rapid action, but the problem is costly and difficult to address. Over time, the public and the media lose interest, and the problem gradually fades from the public consciousness, often unresolved. Any recurrences of publicity are often brief, having lost their novelty factor.

So has the environmental movement been a success? Have its members achieved their goals? These are questions that are only now being asked about what is still a comparatively young movement. Clearly, many individual campaigns have been successful, overcoming sustained resistance to bring about laws and industrial standards that protect rivers, air quality and the wider environment, especially in the West.

The environmental movement now faces the challenge of the internationalisation of environmental issues and policy. Both the causes and effects of environmental problems such as climate change are global in character. To tackle problems of this complexity, environmental groups and the wider movement will have to work together in a 'green coalition' to secure a worldwide call for action. A new global generation of grassroots groups will be central to providing the power and legitimacy this green coalition needs. They will need to bring new ideas, new tactics, and crucially the ability to re-energise the environmental movement by empowering individuals to take action that contributes to a wider international movement.

3 Global environmental governance

In the immediate aftermath of the Second World War, international debate and action were dominated by concerns over world peace, economic development and the elimination of colonialism. Environmental issues were framed by these concerns; developed world economies focused on resource security and scarcity while newly emerging countries sought to protect resource sovereignty. The international community first recognised the deterioration of the environment as an issue that required attention in its own right at the 1972 UN Conference on the Human Environment (UNCHE), held in Stockholm (Sweden). This provided a catalyst for the introduction of multilateral environmental agreements (MEAs) and initiated the modern era of global environmental governance.

Since the UNCHE, the UN has acted as the facilitator of global conferences and agreements on the environment. Its focus and ability to promote action on environmental issues has been influenced largely by the relationships between its more and less powerful member states. During the Cold War, splits were common between the USA and its allies (the first world), the Soviet bloc (the second world) and a large number of poorer, non-aligned developing nations (the third world). After the Cold War, a decade of US dominance shaped the outcomes of a series of global environmental conferences and agreements. Climate change is now at the centre of the global environmental agenda, but negotiations to address this most complex of problems have coincided with the emergence of a new world order. As Brazil, China and India become world powers and experience rapid industrialisation, the future direction of global environmental governance is uncertain.

Resource security and sovereignty

The post-war era of global environmental governance would not have been possible without the initial commitment to multilateralism shown by world powers when they created the UN in 1945. The UN provided a forum through which the global community could discuss, reach consensus and act on global issues. Its early focus was on post-war reconstruction and avoidance of further global conflict, but in 1948 US President Harry S. Truman (1884–1972) proposed a conference to consider the importance of conserving natural resources as a 'major basis for peace'.[1] This proposal was acted on by the UN Economic and Social Council, and in 1949 the UN Scientific Conference on the Conservation and Utilization of Resources (UNSCCUR) was held at Lake Success in New York.[2] The conference was divided into sections on land, water, forests, wildlife and fish, fuels and energy, and minerals. It was attended by 640 scientists and experts from fifty countries. The Soviet Union boycotted the conference, which did not have the power to make recommendations or reach international agreements, but was described at the time as 'the first step by the United Nations towards mobilising the science of the whole world to promote higher standards of living.'[3]

The UN also provided a forum for less economically developed nations to emphasise their sovereignty by pushing for recognition of their rights over domestic natural resources. In 1962 developing nations, led by Chile, secured a UN Declaration on Permanent Sovereignty over Natural Resources.[4] This was followed by a 1966 UN General Assembly Resolution, which recognised that developing nations must be able to exploit and market their natural wealth.[5] The Resolution reflected the increasing voice of developing nations at the UN as membership grew from fifty-one states in 1945 to 122 states by 1967, forty-nine of which were former colonies. By the late 1960s, a G77/China grouping was formally established to harmonise the negotiating priorities of developing countries. This grouping became instrumental in emphasising the links between the global environment and development agendas over the following decades.

International acknowledgement of environmental problems as distinct from resource-use issues arose during the late 1960s. The first major signs of this new environmental focus were displayed at the 1968 Biosphere Conference held in Paris. This UNESCO-organised conference examined the scientific basis for rational use and conservation of the resources of the biosphere, and in doing so discussed the causes of environmental deterioration. Conference delegates expressed concerns over rapid population growth, urbanisation and industrialisation, and these were outlined in a report published the following year by UN Secretary General Thant (1909–74). The report, entitled *Problems of the Human Environment* (1969), suggested the world had a decade to seriously address air and water pollution, soil erosion and the waste of natural resources, and it made newspaper headlines across the world.[6] In doing so it joined a trend for doomsday predictions in a series of books, including *The Population Bomb* (Paul Ehrlich, 1968) and *The Limits to Growth* (Meadows *et al.*, 1972) (see Chapter 5). As public concern over the environment spread, especially in Europe and North America, national governments responded by placing the environment on the global agenda.

UN Conference on the Human Environment

The idea of convening a global conference on the human environment was first proposed by Sweden, which was respected internationally as a neutral and progressive country, and had made considerable contributions to disarmament and development aid. On 13 December 1967, the Swedish Deputy Permanent Secretary, Börje Billner, put forward the idea to the UN General Assembly that a conference be held to facilitate coordination and to focus the interest of member countries on extremely complex problems related to the human environment.[7] The environment summit was proposed as an alternative to holding a fourth international conference on the peaceful use of atomic energy, which was considered expensive and benefiting only the developed countries. At its twenty-third session in December 1968, the UN General Assembly supported the Swedish proposal and agreed it would take place in Stockholm. The General Assembly adopted resolution 2398 (XXIII) convening the UNCHE and noting the '[...] continuing and accelerating impairment of the quality of the human environment' and its 'consequent effects on the condition of man, his physical, mental and social well-being, his dignity and his enjoyment of basic human rights, in developing as well as developed countries.'[8,9]

Many developing nations were initially reluctant to participate in the conference and saw it as an initiative that would jeopardise their potential to exploit domestic natural resources and thus threaten their economic development.[10] They contested the purpose of the conference and the importance of environmental issues as a global priority. As part of the UNCHE preparatory process, intellectuals from developing nations were invited to discuss issues related to the conference agenda.[11] The outcome of these discussions was *The Founex Report on Development and Environment* (1971), which clearly set out the link between environment and development priorities and helped to convince developing countries that environmental issues were relevant to their situation.[12,13] A further challenge was provided by the refusal of the Soviet bloc (except Romania) to attend the conference because of the lack of international recognition of East Germany. Ultimately this did not harm the conference, as developing countries were able to play a central role and present their perspectives on global environmental issues. After nine days of discussion and negotiation, the conference produced an action plan consisting of 106 recommendations, and a Declaration of twenty-six principles on the human environment. This represented unprecedented international agreement, between 113 developing and developed nations, on the environmental problems that should be addressed and the action needed to ensure international cooperation. The conference generated a degree of enthusiasm for environmental action that has had a lasting influence on global environmental governance. Following the conference, Brazil's delegate returned home and convinced his government to create a secretariat for the environment,[14] and a number of other national governments created departments for the environment or introduced domestic environmental legislation.[15] UNCHE also led to the establishment of the UN Environment Programme (UNEP) and provided momentum for an intensive period of international environmental law-making.

UNEP was created to provide a global voice for the environmental agenda within the UN system. Other UN agencies, such as the Food and Agricultural Organization (FAO), World Meteorological Organization (WMO) and World Health Organization (WHO), were all responsible for some aspect of environmental policy. Given the legal autonomy of these agencies, it was decided that existing responsibilities could not be reallocated to UNEP. Some members of the UN also thought that existing agencies were overly bureaucratic, and this resulted in the USA proposing a smaller unit within the UN system that would instil an environmental ethic in other specialised agencies via information, persuasion and direct funding.[16] Because of this, UNEP was established as a programme reporting to the General Assembly and Economic and Social Council rather than a specialised agency. The primary goal of UNEP was to act as a centre for environmental affairs within the UN system and coordinate expertise to address environmental challenges. The secretariat of the new UN Environment Programme was located in Nairobi, Kenya – it was the first and only UN agency to have its headquarters in a developing country. UNEP's location in Kenya sent a message to developing nations that they had a say in the global environmental agenda.

Environment and development

The UNCHE and UNEP started to address the links between the environment and development agendas. However, it took another twenty years for them to be closely aligned on the international stage. A number of high-profile international reports were published in the intervening period that reinforced the idea of global interdependence. These gained widespread coverage at the time of publication and brought the environment and development agendas closer together. In January 1977 the president of the World Bank, Robert McNamara (1916–2009), suggested setting up an international commission to formulate basic proposals to break through an international impasse in negotiations on global development.[17] The Commission was chaired by Willy Brandt (1913–92), the former West German Chancellor, with the aim to influence public opinion, help change government attitudes, and revitalise international engagement between developed countries (the North) and developing countries (the South). The Commission made a case for multilateral engagement on a wide range of international issues. Brandt observed that humankind:

> already faces basic problems which cannot be solved purely at the national or even regional levels, such as security and peace, development goals, the monetary system, protection of the environment, energy, and the control of space and ocean resources. The international community has begun to tackle these problems but, to date, very inadequately.[18]

The membership of the Brandt Commission strongly represented the developing world and covered varying regional and political views. It published two reports, *North–South: A Program for Survival* (1980) and *Common Crisis North–South: Cooperation for World Recovery* (1983). The 1980 *North–South* report outlined a comprehensive strategy for restructuring the global economic order and reinforced the extent of mutual interests on developmental and environmental issues. On publication it became a best-selling book and was published in twenty languages, but a North–South Summit convened to follow up its recommendations was a disappointment and failed to yield firm action.[19] Meanwhile, the global economic outlook was bleak, a debt crisis enveloped much of the developing world, and developed economies experienced massive unemployment. As economic conditions worsened, Brandt and his colleagues published *Common Crisis*, an emergency programme for action that called for a substantial increase in the flow of resources to the developing world. Much was made of the Brandt Reports at the time, but a US-led free market consensus mapped out a different set of actions. Developing countries seeking a way out of the debt crisis were presented with IMF- and World Bank-imposed structural adjustment programmes as a condition for lending and for development aid. These were highly unpopular in developing countries and evidence emerged over time that they had harmful social and environmental impacts.

The UN was routinely marginalised by the USA and other powers during this period, but remained a forum for the expression of environmental, economic and social concerns. In 1983, the same year that *Common Crisis* was published, the UN General Assembly passed Resolution 38/161,[20] establishing the World Commission on Environment and Development (WCED). The Norwegian Prime Minister, Gro Harlem Brundtland (b. 1939), chaired the Commission, and its report, *Our Common Future*, also known as the Brundtland Report, was published in 1987. *Our Common Future* went further than any publication before it in reframing the link between environment and development. To do this it defined the requirements for 'sustainable development', a concept that had been introduced seven years earlier in the *World Conservation Strategy* (1980) published by a coalition of UN agencies and environmental groups.[21] The *World Conservation Strategy* stressed the interdependence of conservation and development and emphasised that for development to be sustainable it must 'take account of social and ecological factors, as well as economic ones'[22] The Brundtland Commission elaborated on the ideas of the *World Conservation Strategy* by framing them in an intergenerational context. It defined sustainable development as: 'development that meets the needs of the present without compromising the ability of future generations to meet their own needs.' It highlighted three fundamental components to sustainable development: environmental protection, economic growth and social equity.[23]

During the lifetime of the Commission a number of international environmental disasters occurred, including the 1984 Union Carbide chemical explosion at Bhopal in India; the 1986 Chernobyl nuclear power plant disaster in the Soviet Union; and toxic chemical spills in the Rhine River.[24] These placed the spotlight on the environmental behaviour of industry and contributed to a revived global consciousness of environmental issues. One of the Brundtland Commission's recommendations was the convening of a global conference in the mould of UNCHE. This led to the 1992 UN Conference on Environment and Development (UNCED), also known as the 'Earth Summit', which was held on the 3–12 June in Rio de Janeiro, Brazil, twenty years after the Stockholm Conference.

The Rio Earth Summit

UNCED was one of the most publicised large-scale political events since the end of the Cold War.[25] A total of 172 countries and over 100 heads of state were represented at the conference. In addition 17,000 people including approximately 2400 representatives of non-governmental organisations (NGOs) attended the parallel NGO Global Forum.[26] Developing countries came to the Rio Summit with a greater willingness to participate in the global environmental policy-making process than they had shown twenty years earlier in Stockholm, but the Summit highlighted the complexity of the global environmental challenge. Negotiations on climate change, biodiversity and the world's forests proved to be contentious. Developing nations complained that developed nations were reluctant to commit the funds required for new measures, while campaign groups pushed for further consideration of consumption and the behaviour of multinational corporations as drivers of environmental destruction. Before the Conference, US President George H. Bush gave a speech promising the American public that American jobs came before the environment. During the conference, the US delegation insisted that no date should be fixed to reduce greenhouse gases to 1990 levels in the climate change convention. Other nations sought to protect their own interests. In the preparatory process, Arab oil nations attempted to remove energy conservation from the Agenda 21 plan of action. The UK was criticised for its opposition to the UN target for developed nations to give 0.7 per cent of national income to development aid.[27] The Pearson Commission originally proposed the overseas aid target in 1969, and this was reiterated by the Brandt Report a decade later. With regard to forestry, the Summit failed to agree a legally binding convention to protect the world's forests. Developing nations, led by Malaysia and India, argued that such a convention might interfere with their sovereign right to exploit forest resources.[28]

UNCED negotiators eventually secured the adoption of the UN Framework Convention on Climate Change (UNFCCC); the Convention on Biological Diversity (CBD); a global plan of action to promote sustainable development called Agenda 21; the Rio Declaration on Environment and Development, which set out a series of principles defining the rights and responsibilities of states; and a Statement of Forest Principles to support the sustainable management of the world's forests. The Summit also established the Commission on Sustainable Development (CSD) to monitor progress on the implementation of Agenda 21, and a funding mechanism called the Global Environment Facility (GEF), which would be managed by the World Bank. At its close, Maurice Strong, the Conference Secretary-General, called the Summit a 'historic moment for humanity'. Although Agenda 21 had been weakened by compromise and negotiation, he said, it was still the most comprehensive and, if implemented, effective programme of action ever sanctioned by the international community.[29]

The optimism of the Post-Rio era, although not universal, was influenced by a number of factors. These included the end of the Cold War and a broad consensus that environment and development needs could be reconciled. The parallel Global Forum had been a catalyst for civil society networking and concerted transnational advocacy, and provided a model for other global conferences.[30] UNCED influenced a series of subsequent UN conferences, which examined population (1994), social development (1995), rights and roles of women (1995) and human settlements (1996).[31]

In 1997, the UN General Assembly held a special session on the environment (also known as Rio+5) to review and appraise the implementation of Agenda 21. During this session, member states called for sustainable development efforts to focus on the eradication of poverty as an overriding priority, stating: 'The enormity and complexity of the poverty issue could very well endanger the social fabric, undermine economic development and the environment, and threaten political stability in many countries.' The session's final document (Resolution S-19/2) outlined the need for a high-profile conference, equal in scale and ambition to UNCED, to bring about genuine progress on this agenda. The need for action was further highlighted in December 2000, when the UN General Assembly adopted Resolution 55/199, acknowledging that, despite many successful and continuing efforts of the international community since UNCHE, the environment and the natural resource base continued to deteriorate at an alarming rate. Following this, the UN convened a World Summit on Sustainable Development (WSSD) to reinvigorate the global commitment to sustainable development and undertake a ten-year review of progress achieved since 1992.

The WSSD (also known as Rio+10) was held in Johannesburg (South Africa) from 26 August to 4 September 2002, and was attended by approximately 100 world leaders and over 22,000 participants. However, the decision by US President George W. Bush not to attend the summit rendered it partially impotent. A year earlier, Bush had rejected the Kyoto Protocol to tackle climate change, claiming that it would cripple the US economy and that it gave unfair exemptions to developing nations. Many saw the US position as increasingly isolationist and out of step with international concerns.[32] The Secretary of State, Colin Powell, led the US delegation, which emphasised deals with the private sector and stressed the importance of economic growth over binding global treaties to fight environmental problems and poverty. Powell was jeered by protestors on the final day of the Summit, accusing the USA of blocking meaningful action on a blueprint to protect the planet.

Whereas the UNCED focused on the state of the planet, WSSD focused on socio-economic development within the context of environmental stewardship. In particular, the summit concentrated on an action plan of deliverables across the areas of water and sanitation, energy, health, agriculture and biodiversity (WEHAB). Due to the host country being South Africa, there was a deliberate attempt to connect WEHAB to the Millennium Development Goals (MDGs) and the New Partnership for Africa's Development (NEPAD) initiative.[33] As well as poverty, the Summit recognised the increasing importance of globalisation. While the rapid integration of markets, mobility of capital and increases in investment flows around the world had provided new opportunities, they also provided new challenges for sustainable development. The costs and benefits of globalisation have been unevenly distributed, with developing countries in particular struggling to achieve sustainable development.

The outcome of the Summit was its Plan of Implementation and the Johannesburg Declaration on Sustainable Development. Unlike previous global conferences, WSSD did not set out international principles that could be invoked in legal or political contexts. Fearful that conventional intergovernmental diplomacy was unlikely to result in action, the Summit promoted multi-stakeholder Type II partnerships between governments, citizen groups and businesses to implement sustainable development goals. They were an alternative to Type I partnerships, the traditional intergovernmental partnerships that often marked the outcome of international treaties.

WSSD temporarily raised the profile of sustainable development. Although its impact was less substantial than that of UNCHE or UNCED, it furthered the integration of the global environmental and development agendas. Each of these conferences provided a rallying point for global environmentalism and placed it firmly on the environmental agenda. The long-lasting global environmental governance frameworks they brought about illustrate their legacy.

Instruments of global environmental governance

Multilateral environmental agreements (MEAs) are legally binding instruments between two or more nation states that deal with some aspect of the environment. Over 300 have been created since UNCHE, with UNEP taking an active role in initiating many of them.[34] Early

MEAs covered specific traditional conservation issues such as the protection of wetlands (Ramsar Convention, 1971) or of endangered species (Convention on International Trade in Endangered Species of Wild Fauna and Flora, CITES, 1973). From the late 1980s onwards, MEAs were established to address a wide range of second-generation environmental issues, including ozone-depleting substances (Vienna Convention, 1985; Montreal Protocol, 1987); hazardous wastes (Basel Convention, 1989); climate change (UNFCCC, 1992); hazardous chemicals and pesticides (Rotterdam Convention, 1998); bio-safety (Cartagena Protocol, 2000); and persistent organic pollutants (Stockholm Convention, 2001). MEAs have also proved important for the management of the global commons (various conventions on conservation of the Antarctic) and regional issues (there are seventeen regional seas conventions).

A large number of nations have shown a willingness to sign major global MEAs – many have well over 100 signatories – but the success of their implementation is more difficult to measure. They are often initiated with some urgency after global environmental issues have been identified, but negotiations to agree them can take years. Framework conventions are commonly agreed as a first step without binding agreements. They are then reviewed and tightened over time. The most successful MEAs have worked because it has clearly been in the interest of the international community to support them. The Montreal Protocol on Substances that Deplete the Ozone Layer is widely cited as environmental multilateralism at its most effective. Public concern over the health and environmental impacts of depletion of the ozone layer first translated into coordinated international action in 1985, when twenty nations signed the Vienna Convention for the Protection of the Ozone Layer. This was a framework agreement which established a platform for the negotiation of international regulations on ozone-depleting substances. That same year the British Antarctic Survey found that the springtime atmospheric concentration of ozone in the Antarctic had decreased by 40 per cent from 1964 levels. The US Environmental Protection Agency also estimated that a 50 per cent reduction in chlorofluorocarbon (CFC) emissions from 1986 levels could save the US trillions of dollars in reduced health costs associated with treating skin cancer. By 1987, representatives from forty-three nations had agreed to sign the Montreal Protocol, freeze production of CFCs at 1986 levels, and reduce production by 50 per cent by 1999. As further scientific evidence about the ozone layer was published, the Protocol was strengthened in 1990 and again in 1992 to phase out CFCs entirely by 1996. CFCs stay in the atmosphere for a long time, but the Montreal Protocol has led to reductions in the atmospheric concentrations of ozone-depleting compounds after a peak in 1994. This success story can be attributed in part to supportive institutional and economic conditions. At the time of signing the Protocol, just twelve countries emitted 78 per cent of emissions; the USA was among them and was prepared to take an international lead. Most producers of CFCs had diversified product portfolios and were able to adapt to a ban on CFCs as substitutes were quickly discovered and brought to market. The risk of CFC production was also understood as a health issue, though many environmental groups campaigned actively on the issue. Taken together, the conditions were right for international agreement.[35]

MEAs encounter problems when they are subject to scientific uncertainty, and require universal support from the international community but are seen to threaten economic interests. The history of the UNFCCC includes all these factors and more. Today, the global implications of acting or not acting on climate change give it a greater importance than any other environmental issue. The inability of the international community to form a binding, effective agreement consequently raises questions about the future of MEAs.

International climate change negotiations are supported by institutional apparatus designed to bring about scientific and political consensus. The scientific support is provided by the Intergovernmental Panel on Climate Change (IPCC), created in 1988 by the WMO and UNEP. The IPCC's aims are to assess information on the causes of climate change, its impacts, and options for addressing them. It produced its first assessment report on the science of climate change in 1990, and its findings supported the establishment of the main apparatus for negotiations: the UNFCCC.

Global climate change policy

Since 1990 four IPCC assessment reports have been produced, each providing new and stronger evidence that global warming can be attributed to human activities. The IPCC's second assessment report, published in 1995, concluded that 'the balance of evidence suggests a discernible human influence on global climate'.[36] By the fourth assessment report (2007), the IPCC's conclusions were more strongly worded:

> Most of the observed increase in globally averaged temperatures since the mid-20th century is very likely due to the observed increase in anthropogenic (human) greenhouse gas concentrations.[37]

The scientific and intergovernmental nature of the IPCC was designed to provide the international community with balanced information that could provide the evidence for political action. Its assessment helped drive the international agenda. In 2007, the IPCC was awarded the Nobel Peace Prize for its 'efforts to lay the foundations for measures that are needed to counteract climate change'.[38] This degree of scientific coordination could be regarded as a model for supporting MEAs, but opponents of a global agreement have used scientific uncertainty to justify inaction. There are many reasons for the long drawn-out nature of climate change negotiations, but these are primarily economic, not scientific, as the Kyoto process demonstrated.

After the first IPCC assessment report, countries acted quickly to adopt the UNFCCC in 1992. The UNFCCC provided a framework for negotiating protocols that would set mandatory greenhouse gas limits. Its non-binding status meant it was ratified by a large number of countries including the USA, and entered into force in 1994. From 1995 onwards, all signatories of the UNFCCC have met at annual Conferences of the Parties (COP) to further refine the treaty. COP 3 in 1997 established the Kyoto Protocol to create mandatory emissions-reduction targets for specific developed countries to be achieved by 2008–12. The major area of contention between developing and developed countries negotiating the Kyoto Protocol was the allocation of responsibility for cutting atmospheric greenhouse gas emissions. All nations produce emissions linked to a wide range of economic activities. The destruction of rainforests and burning of 'dirty' fuels by power stations are major causes of emissions in developing economies. Developed nations have higher per capita emissions, driven by energy use in the home and private transport. International trade has complicated matters as many of the goods consumed in developed nations are produced in developing countries and generate emissions. The distinction between historical, current and projected emissions is also important. The USA and Europe generated over 50 per cent of carbon dioxide emissions in the twentieth century as their economies developed. But over the past decade China has overtaken the USA as the single biggest emitter of carbon dioxide emissions and is still an economy in transition, with further economic growth needed to raise millions out of poverty. The Kyoto Protocol was designed to address these issues through the application of common but differential responsibilities. Thirty-seven industrial nations were classified as Annex 1 countries and set individual targets to cut emissions by, on average, 5 per cent below 1990 levels by 2008–12. Developing nations were excluded from mandatory emissions cuts, but after 2012 a new set of targets for nations was expected. This arrangement recognised that developed nations, as historical polluters, must bear the immediate cost for addressing climate change, but the USA in particular was concerned that the costs to its economy would be too high. As a consequence, many countries stalled ratification or, as in the case of the USA, refused to ratify it at all. Overall, Kyoto took eight years to come into force.

By 2007, emissions data from Annex 1 countries showed many of them had failed to reduce their emissions on a year-on-year basis. Criticism of the level of cuts achieved by developed nations was only partly ameliorated by an announcement from G8 nations that they would aim to at least halve global carbon dioxide emissions by 2050. With the Kyoto Protocol nearing the end of its life span, attention turned towards negotiating a new set of international targets, either through an extension to Kyoto or as a successor to it. COP 13 in Bali, Indonesia and COP 14 in Poznan, Poland focused on laying the foundations for the agreement of a new climate change agreement at COP 15 in Copenhagen, Denmark. When COP 15 took place in December 2009, it had all the characteristics of an environmental 'mega conference'. A total of 10,500 delegates, 13,500 observers and 3000 media representatives attended COP 15, while 120 of the world's leaders were scheduled to arrive in time for a final agreement. Many attendees were hopeful, as the election of US President Barack Obama raised the possibility of US agreement to legally binding targets, a move that was essential in order for other major economies to do a deal. Others were desperate; an Alliance of Small Island States expressed their grave concern that climate change posed the most serious threat to their survival and viability. Controversy over the scientific methods employed by scientists involved in the IPCC process beset the preparations for the conference (see Chapter 4). For a number of weeks, these and many other climate change issues dominated the global news agenda.

Part of the reason for the high profile of COP 15 was that it was purposely and publicly used as a target for an international agreement to focus negotiators' minds. UNCHE and UNCED in particular had worked in this way before, by pressing the international community to make the compromises needed to reach an agreement that could be announced as a conference success. Developed economies wanted a new protocol that included developing countries and recognised that economies such as Brazil, China and India were now major polluters. In particular China, the EU, India and the USA could not reach agreement on the core elements of a binding agreement. The final outcome was a statement of commitment to action called the

Copenhagen Accord, supplemented by an annex of non-binding commitments from all the major polluting countries. Developed nations also made funding commitments to support developing countries in mitigating climate change, with a particular focus on halting deforestation. These were significant developments in their own right but not the binding commitment that so many wanted.

Commentators have provided a long list of reasons why COP 15 failed to produce the agreement that had been hoped for. Some blamed separate but parallel negotiations, which divided those who wanted an extension of the Kyoto Protocol (developing nations) and those who wanted to replace it (developed nations). Others suggested the UN processes needed overhauling, or blamed the Danish host's conference facilitation. President Obama made it clear he had limited political capital to spend, as opposition to his healthcare legislation dominated US politics. China opposed US demands to monitor emission reductions, and on one occasion during negotiations sent a junior diplomat to talks with world leaders. Meanwhile, the EU stepped back from committing to improve its emissions targets for 2020, a move that could have stimulated action by other major powers.

Following COP 15, climate talks continued through 2010. In early December 2010, the international community convened at COP 16 in Cancun, Mexico. Negotiations were constructive and dealt with some of the issues COP 15 had not resolved. Countries agreed principles for monitoring, reporting and verification of emissions, and established a Green Climate Fund for channelling mitigation and adaptation funding to developing nations. They also formally submitted their emissions reductions targets under the UNFCCC process, building on the Copenhagen Accord's hastily collected commitments. These outcomes were relatively modest but reinstated some measure of trust in the UN-led process among the international community. Although emissions-reduction targets remained voluntary, the negotiation process was able to move forward with the aim of a more comprehensive agreement at COP 17 in Durban, South Africa in 2011.

Understanding global environmental governance

This chapter has examined the emergence of global environmental governance from the first international summit to address human environment issues in 1972 to the current international negotiations on a post-Kyoto treaty to reduce greenhouse gas emissions and tackle climate change. During this time, the international environmental agenda has evolved to include economic development and poverty alleviation.

While there has been a dramatic increase in the number of environmental institutions, policies and programmes, the current governance framework has been hampered by structural shortcomings and continual mistrust between developed and developing nations. Global environmental agreements are based on thousands of hours of technical negotiations. The process by which they are put together has been criticised as undemocratic because developing countries with limited resources are not able to participate in all the decisions.

UNEP has acted as a global-level advocate for the environment. It has been successful in establishing international agreements that have led to international standards, policies and guidelines on endangered species, migratory wild animals, protection of the ozone layer, transboundary movement of waste, biodiversity, desertification, and persistent organic pollutants. Most of these international agreements have become autonomous entities, each with its own secretariat, and many have become more influential than UNEP itself.

Despite UNEP's success in creating environmental agreements, it has faced challenges in coordinating international environmental action and has failed to fulfil some of its core functions effectively.[39] Critics of the current global environmental governance system have called for its reform and a clearer division of responsibilities among institutions, or centralisation of the current system under one umbrella of a 'world environment organisation'.

Global environmental governance has now reached a critical juncture, with climate change negotiations and preparation for the 2012 Earth Summit (Stockholm +40, Rio +20) being undertaken to the backdrop of a global economic downturn and geopolitical shifts in power. Numerous countries now have the ability to make or break international agreements. China, the EU, Brazil, India, Japan and the USA each represent power bases that can, and do, act unilaterally to protect their own interests.[40] This has led some to speculate that action on climate change in particular will shift further from global political cooperation towards national economic competition focused on low carbon growth (see Chapter 5).[41] For the international community to take further action on global environmental issues, an institutional framework will be needed that holds the international community together and addresses the distinct views of not one, not two, but all centres of global power.

4 Science and the environment

Environmentalism has a strong scientific basis that sets it apart from other ideologies. At its heart is a fascination with the natural world, how it works, and how it relates to humankind that can be traced back through history. Today ecological ideas inform the language and belief systems of many environmentalists, though ecological principles can lead to very different conclusions about how society, the economy and the environment should interact. Scientific information has also highlighted the scale of modern environmental problems. Since the publication of Rachel Carson's *Silent Spring* (1962), the use of scientific evidence has become one of the central ways in which environmental arguments have been constructed. It is now essential for environmental policies to be evidence-based – the case for action backed by science. However, this modern-day reliance on science has coincided with the emergence of environmental problems that are highly complex in nature and characterised by uncertainty. Over recent decades, scientific evidence has been challenged, misunderstood or wilfully misinterpreted. Today, the ability of scientific evidence to settle debates over issues such as climate change is deeply compromised.

The study of nature

The earliest surviving studies of the environment were produced during the classical period: Aristotle (384–322 BC) and Theophrastus (*c*. 371–*c*. 287 BC) classified and described the natural world and Hippocrates (*c*. 460–*c*. 370 BC) depicted the impact of climate on human health. Later, the Roman Pliny the Elder (AD 23–79) wrote *Historia Naturalis*, an encyclopaedia which sought to catalogue all the entities found in nature.[1] These classical works remained a reference point as the exploration of the natural world evolved. For centuries, Europeans treated the world as a mystery created by God, and the study of nature reflected this. The English naturalist John Ray (1627–1705) called his popular study of the natural world *The Wisdom of God Manifested in the Works of the Creation* (1691) and the Swedish naturalist Carl Linnaeus (1707–78) attributed his system of classifying species of plants and animals to God's design. Like other enlightenment thinkers, Linnaeus and Ray sought to make the world understandable through scientific exploration which resulted in the development of new rules, explanations and theories. In *Systema Naturae* (1758), Linnaeus classified humans next to monkeys in the animal kingdom. This scientific classification placed humans within rather than apart from nature and thus introduced an idea that has become central to modern ecological thinking.

Many other ecological ideas were developed during the enlightenment period. Pehr Kalm (1716–79) studied with Linnaeus and later travelled in North America, where he linked a decline in the abundance of wildlife to settlers' hunting techniques. The explorer and naturalist Alexander von Humboldt (1769–1859) combined the physical and natural sciences to explain the impact of terrain and climate on plants. Thomas Malthus (1766–1834) set out how population growth was mediated by limits to resources, and Charles Darwin (1809–82) developed his theory of evolution. In the 1860s, Ernst Haeckel (1834–1919) introduced the term 'ecology' to describe the relations between organisms and their environment. In the same decade, George Perkins Marsh (1801–82) published *Man and Nature* (1864), and argued that humankind was the prime cause of species extinction.[2]

As nineteenth-century scientific thinking introduced a new understanding of ecological processes, these were used to support ideas related to the ordering of the economy and of society. Henry Thoreau's (1817–62) exploration of the land surrounding Walden Pond near Concord, Massachusetts in the USA informed his appreciation of natural simplicity, and his views on the ties between people and nature drew upon his understanding of local ecology.[3] The Russian anarchist communist Peter Kropotkin (1842–1921) developed ideas about self-sufficiency, local organisation and production based on his studies of animal behaviour. In his book *Mutual Aid: A Factor of Evolution* (1902), he used examples from the animal world to show how cooperation rather than competition was central to societal prosperity and progress. No clear-cut scientific tradition or political philosophy emerges from these examples, but by the early twentieth century enough scientists were studying the relationship between organisms and their environment for this to be recognised as a specific field of study. In 1913 the British Ecological Society held its inaugural meeting, followed two years later by the foundation of the Ecological Society of America. Soon ecological ideas were applied to forest and fisheries management and to agriculture but they did not immediately transfer to the public sphere. The forester and academic Aldo Leopold (1886–1948) was one of the first to combine ecological ideas with aesthetic and ethical values in a way that clearly chimes with contemporary environmental thinking. Leopold set out a land ethic that emphasised harmony between humans, soils, water, plants and animals as a single community. In *A Sand County Almanac* he wrote 'a thing is right when it tends to preserve the integrity, beauty, and stability of the biotic community. It is wrong when it tends otherwise.'[4] This philosophy gained wider appeal from the late 1960s as momentous changes in social, economic and political conditions combined with rapid and visible changes in the state of the environment.

The control of nature

Over the past half-century, fascination with the natural world has been combined with concern over how much resource use and pollution the environment can assimilate. Scientific identification of changes in the natural environment, and diagnosis of their causes, have played a central role in highlighting environmental issues to the wider public. At the same time, scientific advances have facilitated the increased rate and scale of environmental change. The Second World War brought about massive changes in technology, which were utilised in peacetime to secure economic prosperity. Chemical pesticides deployed during the war to control disease found a ready market as products to eradicate pests on farmland and in people's homes. Ecological sciences benefited from and were brought into this industrial expansion; funding brought new scientific apparatus and the opportunity to use quantitative techniques and modelling; and ecologists were employed by government agencies to improve the use and management of natural resources.

The increased use of chemical pesticides and the concern of scientists over their wider impacts were central to the development of modern environmentalism, particularly in the USA. Given the great benefits of increased agricultural production and pest control, it took some time for concerns about them to reach the public consciousness. In the 1940s and 1950s there were signs that chemical use could affect non-target species, but this was not scientifically well understood. In the UK, large-scale bird and fox deaths were raised in the House of Lords. In the USA, scientists challenged indiscriminate aerial spraying, but between 1947 and 1960 domestic production of synthetic pesticides increased more than fivefold. By the late 1950s, more wildlife conservation and management authorities perceived the need to play an active role in understanding and reducing pesticide hazards. A scientific study for the Californian Fisheries and Game Department played a considerable part in stimulating awareness of the need to act among both the international science community and the American public. In 1960, Hunt and Bischoff published a paper entitled 'Inimical Effects on Wildlife of Periodic DDD Applications to Clear Lake'. It investigated the impact of dichlorodiphenyldichloroethane (DDD), an insecticide closely related to DDT, that was used between 1949 and 1957 to eradicate gnats on a recreational lake north of San Francisco. The Clear Lake study showed that chemicals applied directly to a body of water in low concentrations could progress up the natural food chain in ever greater concentrations, even when no trace could be found in the water shortly after application. Over a number of years and repeated applications, DDD transferred up the food chain from plankton to fish and frogs and then to grebes and gulls. The population of grebes at Clear Lake fell from over 1000 pairs to approximately thirty in 1960.

Shortly after the paper was published, it was brought to the attention of Norman Moore (b. 1923), the head of the Nature Conservancy's newly established Toxic Chemicals and Wildlife research station at Monks Wood in the UK. Moore had been struggling with the problem of which pesticide to prioritise for research in the UK. The Clear Lake study convinced him of the importance of studying pesticides with a highly persistent nature, and shaped the direction of UK research into toxic chemicals for years to come.[5] The Clear Lake study also came to the attention of the biologist and writer Rachel Carson (1907–64) as she gathered research on the widespread use of pesticides. Carson had been concerned about the impact of pesticides for many years and was in the process of synthesising a mass of scientific evidence and case studies for a book intended for a wide public audience. The central chapters of the book focused on the widespread use of DDT, but the text as a whole named and documented the impact of a wide range of chemicals. Carson used the Clear Lake study to illustrate the unstated risk of 'this whole chain of poisoning' to communities who fished or took water from lakes and rivers.[6] The completed work was first serialised in the *New Yorker* and then published in book form as *Silent Spring* in 1962. In the USA, *Silent Spring* was a popular science phenomenon – almost a million copies were sold in its first two years. As pesticide use rose up the political agenda, Carson was interviewed on news programmes and testified to a subcommittee of the US Senate. Pesticide industry groups lobbied against her work but many other scientists publicly supported her. As a consequence, US President John F. Kennedy ordered his Science Advisory Committee to examine pesticide use (see Chapter 2).

Silent Spring was not simply a book about pesticides: it translated fundamental ecological principles into clear environmental messages, and it challenged big business and the idea that science could be used to control nature. Before Carson completed the book, she wrote to a friend:

> I told you that a possible opening sentence had drifted to the surface of my mind recently. It was 'this is a book about a man's war against nature, and because man is part of nature it is also and inevitably a book about man's war against himself.'[7]

In the end Carson did not use this opening, but she wrote vividly about 'man's assaults upon the environment', describing pesticides as 'elixirs of death'. When *Silent Spring* was published against the backdrop of the Cuban missile crisis and the use of chemical herbicides in the Vietnam War, it found a scared, outraged and receptive public. As concern for the future of the planet and humanity grew, more people equated the environment with radical and alternative ideas for the ordering of society.

Radical ecology

In 1969, billboard adverts appeared across Vancouver with the message 'Ecology? Look it up! You're involved'. Ben Metcalfe (1919–2003), a journalist who later became the first chairman of Greenpeace, paid for the posters as he wanted to promote ecology as a revolutionary idea.[8] The following year, Edward Goldsmith (1928–2009) published the first edition of a new magazine called *The Ecologist* as a platform for environmental thinking in the UK. The magazine reached a wide audience in 1972 when it published Goldsmith's 'A Blueprint for Survival', a manifesto for societal change that was endorsed by scientists and academics and went on to sell 750,000 copies as a paperback book. For Metcalfe and Goldsmith, ecology was not solely a field of science, it was a philosophy to live by, one that challenged the assumptions and practices of modern society. As groups and individuals developed numerous environmental philosophies, some ecological ideas became a constant: all forms of life, including humans, are interdependent; the Earth's resources are limited and finite; modern human activities risk damaging the environment at a scale that cannot be recovered from; and by damaging the environment, humanity endangers itself. Each of these ideas challenged accepted patterns of economic growth, technological progress and modern living. For these reasons, the ecologist Paul Sears (1891–1990) described ecology as 'a subversive subject', observing that 'by its very nature, ecology affords a critique of man's operations within the ecosystem'.[9]

Ecology has led to very different ideas about the position and behaviour of humankind within the natural world. The distinctions between these ideas are not widely understood by the public but have been classified in many different ways by academics and writers. Some human-centred approaches hold that rational ecological management of the natural world will enable humanity to prosper, so placing an emphasis on enlightened self-interest. This 'reformist' approach supports the management of the natural environment without questioning the established ordering of society and economy. The creation of environmental protection agencies from the 1970s onwards reflected this managerial approach to environmentalism. Murray Bookchin (1921–2006) developed a more politically revolutionary approach, in which he combined anarchist political philosophy with ecology in books such as *Post-Scarcity Anarchism* (1970). Bookchin's radical ecology described how human relationships with nature depended on, indeed required, an improvement in social conditions. Bookchin believed that reformist approaches to environmentalism perpetuated social and environmental crisis by not challenging inequitable socio-economic systems.[10] An alternative approach starts with the natural world, using basic ecological concepts to emphasise the value of nature in its own right and independently of humanity. This viewpoint is often described as 'deep ecology' – a term introduced in the early 1970s by the Norwegian philosopher Arne Naess (1912–2009). This biocentric or Earth-centred approach has often been interpreted as putting nature first, humanity second.

The US National Aeronautics and Space Administration (NASA) scientist James Lovelock (b. 1919) introduced a scientific twist to the biocentric approach to environmentalism when he developed his Gaia hypothesis during the 1970s. Lovelock had been asked by NASA to investigate ways of detecting life on other planets, and had decided to do so by looking at the chemical composition of their atmospheres. In the process he realised that his approach showed the Earth's atmosphere to be so chemically affected by life that, in his words, it 'might be considered as an extension of life'.[11] The idea that living organisms act on their environment and *vice versa* had been long accepted, as had the idea that the planetary environment has been profoundly altered by life. Lovelock took this further by suggesting that the Earth could be considered as a single living system and that life unconsciously regulated the planetary environment to perpetuate its survival. This hypothesis combined a holistic, global-scale science of the environment with a mythical vision of Gaia, the Greek Goddess of the Earth. The Gaia hypothesis has proved controversial among scientists and even some environmentalists. At first Lovelock could not get his ideas published in academic journals, but they have persisted and found new audiences as global environmental challenges such as climate change have come to the fore.

Science in environmental policy

Scientists are expected to identify and diagnose environmental problems and to develop solutions. Most nation states have environment agencies, government departments or elected representatives and use science to inform policy, but forty years ago many of these institutions did not exist. It was not until 1970 that the UK government set up the Royal Commission for Environmental Pollution and a Department for the Environment, and the US administration established the US Environmental Protection Agency. Each of these agencies was established to address growing public concern about the potentially harmful effects of environmental pollution. They were a departure from the forestry, fisheries and agricultural agencies that preceded them in that their primary concern was environmental not economic. Science was fundamental to the ability of these agencies to make an impact on government. Scientific data enabled environmental issues to be described in factual terms that could be perceived as value-free. Numbers helped; they could be compared with economic costs and benefits and they fitted the language of governance.[12] Through this technical process, contemporary environmentalism was institutionalised in its least radical forms. Environmental sciences incorporating ecology and wider natural, physical and social sciences developed quickly to meet the demands of the policy arena. Protection of any aspect of the natural environment required scientists to establish its desired state and its key features at different scales. Methods were developed to describe environmental components' condition, abundance and importance, and their vulnerability to pressures that could change the way they functioned. These methods were applied to policies on air, water, soils, oceans, flora and fauna.

Technological advances over the past fifty years, together with global scientific coordination, have helped scientists to meet policy demands and also to drive environmental policy. In particular, a revolution in global-scale environmental science has pushed new environmental issues to the top of the political agenda. From 1964 onwards, a series of *Nimbus* Earth observation satellites enabled remote sensing of the atmosphere, land surface, oceans and ecosystems. Scientists became able to collect satellite data on water vapour, oceanic temperature and ozone levels in the atmosphere, and computers were becoming powerful enough to apply the data to models. Starting in the late 1960s, the UN system endorsed and supported global collaboration and research programmes such as the Global Atmospheric Research Programme (GARP) and the Global Environment Monitoring System (GEMS).

Over time, communities of scientists developed new data sets and evidence from which globalised fields of science evolved. Conservation biology emerged from the study of biodiversity and species extinction as a field of science in its own right. Whereas Linnaeus classified over 10,000 species in the eighteenth century, modern-day scientists now recognise over 10,000 new species a year.[13] Each new field of science introduced ideas and concepts that could be applied to policy or capture public attention. From 1966 onwards, the International Union for Conservation of Nature (IUCN) published Red Data Books of threatened species in need of conservation attention, and a series of academic papers and studies all pointed towards the threat of biodiversity loss.[14] At the same time, scientific expeditions into inaccessible jungles, deserts and the deep ocean provided stories and images of newly discovered species for television and print media. The term 'biodiversity' came into use in the late 1980s, and by 1992 international momentum led to the adoption of the CBD.

The climate science community followed a similar pattern of development. Modern climate science began with observational programmes of atmospheric concentrations of carbon dioxide in the 1950s. The coordination of global research efforts was driven by meteorological organisations, and the first World Climate Research Programme was established in 1980. The first high-profile study of what might happen to the global climate over time was published in 1986[15] and the IPCC was formed a year later. The IPCC has been credited with establishing an informed scientific community that enabled the science of climate change to evolve rapidly. Through the IPCC's scientific Working Group 1, scientists with different expertise shared ideas and gained a broader picture of how their work related to the issue. This led to the development of models that used relationships between the oceans, atmosphere, sea ice and land surfaces to improve understanding of climate change over time. Between the years 1990 and

2000, the number of articles on climate change published in science journals increased fivefold and governments and the public started to take notice of climate change.[16]

Biodiversity together with climate change secured global attention at the 1992 Rio Earth Summit through the CBD and the UNFCCC (see Chapter 3). These examples show that science has lost none of the power first shown by *Silent Spring* to push scientific issues to the top of the global political agenda. It is when this attention has been secured and a political response is required that science has run into problems. Globally coordinated action on both climate change and biodiversity is behind where scientists say it should be. The 2010 *Global Biodiversity Outlook* found that the target established in 2002 to achieve a significant reduction in the rate of biodiversity loss by 2010 had not been met.[17] Meanwhile there are still challenges facing globally coordinated action on climate change (see Chapter 3).

The contemporary challenges of applying science to environmental policy are manifold, but two particular issues stand out. Firstly, there is a demand for ever-greater levels of conclusive evidence to support action (the burden of proof). Secondly, there is politically motivated abuse and misuse of science, resulting in a decline in its authority (science under fire).

The burden of proof

Over time, the establishment of environmental agencies with the scientific know-how to diagnose and pre-empt environmental problems has led to the creation of industry and farming regulations, product standards, and protected species and areas. Scientific evidence has been central to government-sponsored action to protect the environment, but this has not been without controversy. Typically, the decision to introduce environmental regulations pits the environment against industrial interests. Departments and agencies of government sometimes disagree internally if not publicly on what measures should be introduced. The scientific complexity of environmental issues makes it difficult to prove conclusively any one side of an argument. This lack of conclusive scientific evidence has served to entrench the position of those who favour and oppose environmental action. International debates over acid rain in the 1970s and 1980s, and genetically modified (GM) food in the 1990s and 2000s, exemplify the contrasting ways this scenario has played out. In each example, the debate revolved around two aspects of the burden of proof: which side was responsible for proving their case, and how much evidence they needed to do so.

The problem of acid rain can be traced back to the industrial revolution. Robert Angus Smith (1817–84), Britain's first official air-pollution inspector, monitored the concentration of sulphuric acid in rain near to industrial Manchester and described its effects in his book *Air and Rain* (1872): 'there is no hope for vegetation […] galvanized iron is valueless […] stone and bricks of buildings crumble'.[18] Over the next century, industrialising nations suffered air pollution on a grand scale, and in the UK highly visible pollution events such as the 1952 great London smog brought about public demand for action on smoke pollution and a government-backed enquiry. The resulting *Beaver Committee Report* (1954) concluded that levels of air pollution could no longer be tolerated but also observed that 'sulphur dioxide is one of the most harmful of all polluting agents'.[19] The UK government responded by passing the 1956 Clean Air Act, which established smokeless zones and encouraged the burning of smokeless fuels. A new generation of power stations were built outside cities with tall chimneys to disperse pollutants, but the Beaver Committee's recommendations to install sulphur dioxide-removing measures were considered too costly.

On a localised basis, the link between industrial Manchester and its sulphurous environs could be observed and inferred. When scientists in Scandinavia and North America started to express concern about the disappearance of fish from rivers and lakes in the late 1950s and 1960s, it was not immediately obvious that this was due to acid rain or that its source would be thousands of miles away in another country. Scientists had to prove the link between acidic rainfall events and fish and vegetation deaths over a long period, excluding all other factors. Tracing the source of this acid rain was not only scientifically challenging but also controversial. Sweden funded scientists to investigate the problem, and in 1971 accused its European neighbours of exporting air pollution to Scandinavia. It repeated the accusation as host of the 1972 Stockholm UNCHE (see Chapter 3) at which the UK in particular was singled out for criticism. This prompted a five-year study into acid rain by the Organisation for Economic Co-operation and Development (OECD), in which eleven European countries, including the UK and Sweden, participated (1972–77). The study found the UK was a net exporter of sulphur dioxide and concluded that there was strong evidence that this caused acid rain. Two years later, the US and Canadian governments undertook a similar scientific exercise, concluding that effects on fish, forestry and farming were serious and that the USA was responsible for five times more sulphur emissions than Canada.

Not all countries interpreted these findings in the same way. Scandinavian countries and Canada were net importers of sulphur dioxide emissions and swiftly concluded that action was needed. Germany, though a large emitter of sulphur dioxide, was stung into action by public reaction to the death of much loved national forests and an increasingly vocal green movement. The UK and US governments and their respective coal and electricity authorities took a more sceptical stance and demanded further evidence. At the time they were net exporters of sulphur dioxide emissions and were concerned they would bear the cost of action without necessarily receiving any environmental benefit. UK and US officials introduced a number of different arguments to resist action. Some simply ignored the science; one Ohio governor stated that his state was no more responsible for acid rain than Florida was for hurricanes. Others raised the standard of proof impossibly high: a US coal industry representative asked Canadian scientists to tell him which fish were dying in which lake as a consequence of a specific power plant.[20] The British government also emphasised scientific uncertainty and placed the burden of proof on other countries:

> We see no point in making heroic efforts, at great cost, to control one out of many factors unless there is reasonable expectation that such control would lead to a real improvement in the environment [...] Britain's neighbours cannot expect her to enter upon a crash programme while there is still so much that is speculative in the argument.[21]

By the early 1980s, scientists and civil servants at the UK Department of the Environment were convinced that it was in Britain's interests to reduce sulphur dioxide emissions, but other UK government departments and industry interests opposed them. It was not until 1986 that the British government finally accepted the link between British air pollution and Scandinavian acid rain. An air quality accord between Canada and the USA was signed in 1991 after a change in administration from President Ronald Reagan (1981–89) to President George H. Bush (b. 1924).

In the case of acid rain, the problem of lake and forest deaths had already been identified. Governments were in agreement on the need to establish the causes and understand the effects of acid rain, but were in disagreement over the level of evidence needed to justify action. From the 1990s onwards, the development of GM food offered a different focus on the burden of proof. As a new technology ready for commercial exploitation, its real-world impacts were unknown and potentially irreversible. GM food was regarded as different from previous manipulations of crops and animals because it allowed genes from plants and animals to be spliced together. There were concerns that, once released, GM crops could spread GM characteristics into the wild and endanger food safety. In these circumstances a precautionary approach based on scientific evidence was widely advocated. A standard of proof or scientific test was needed to show there was no unacceptable risk but there was strong disagreement between the US and Europe regarding how this was judged. This resulted in a trade dispute which was mediated by the WTO on legal rather than scientific lines.

In circumstances of scientific uncertainty, policy makers introduce 'pseudo' scientific concepts to support their decisions. In Europe, the precautionary principle has become a central tenet of environmental policy applied to GM food products, and demands a high standard of certainty that they will not have an impact on the environment, placing the burden of proof on GM producers. The EU placed a moratorium on the commercial growing of GM crops on this basis. In the USA, the precautionary principle is regarded as overly restrictive, supporting a centralised planning rather than a free-market approach. Instead, the US Food and Drink Administration (FDA) introduced scientific criteria called substantial equivalence to identify how similar new products were to existing ones. In this case, the fact that a product was GM did not matter; what mattered was whether it was substantially different in structure and content.

To some extent these approaches reflected two different scientific schools of thought. Molecular biologists regarded gene splicing as a highly specific process with manageable impacts. Environmentalists regarded GM crops as an unknown quantity once released into the uncontrolled natural environment.[22] These differing scientific approaches reflected different public concerns about the environment and food, as well as different levels of confidence in food safety regulators, through the 1990s and 2000s. In Europe concern over 'frankenfoods' was high following the 1990s 'mad-cow disease' crisis, which saw a fatal, neurodegenerative disease called bovine spongiform encephalopathy (BSE) affect beef farming, particularly in the UK. Trust in UK food regulators was correspondingly low, while the US FDA enjoyed a good reputation in the 1990s due to its stance on smoking and public health. Consequently American consumers generally accepted the light touch regulation of the FDA, while European consumers demanded the strictest of tests for novel products. In the UK, concerns for the environment were also linked to the modern farming practices with which GM was associated. A decline in farmland birds in the UK was linked to GM monoculture by a writer in *The Times*: 'the year 2020 and the most silent of silent springs, apart from the rustle of genetically engineered oilseed rape, wheat, maize and other "designer" crops nodding in the breeze'.[23] In North America, large-scale intensive farming was more widely accepted as a matter of efficiency and technical advancement. All this meant that European consumers were hostile to GM food before it even reached the market, while US consumers were moderately positive.[24]

Today these positions appear as entrenched as ever. The European moratorium on approving the commercial growing of GM crops came to an end in 2010, but individual nations are still able to decide to keep it in place. UK scientists are no nearer to proving that GM crops are safe as protesters have found and destroyed every crop trial attempted since 2000. However, in the USA most corn, soya and oilseed rape is produced from GM crops. While science has offered a way of resolving these differences, disagreements over how it is applied have persisted. It is difficult to determine how science can assist in addressing this impasse.

Science under fire

Scientific authority has driven societal understanding of the environment. This has been marked by the exaggeration, dramatisation and over-simplification of scientific evidence. Many carefully worded scientific conclusions have been misinterpreted in the media or misused by interest groups. Environmentalists and their opponents have battled to monopolise scientific authority, and to control media interpretations and public preconceptions of environmental issues. As a consequence, trust in individuals and institutions has become as important, if not more so, than the science itself. Whereas the burden of proof placed an emphasis on more science and better scientific evidence, the question of trust challenges the authority of scientists themselves. Today, many forms of debate are used to settle environmental arguments, and many of these undermine science. The battle over the disposal of the Brent Spar oil platform in the North Sea and interpretations of climate science provide two examples of how trust in environmental arguments, backed by science, have come under fire.

From the late 1960s onwards, professional campaign groups employed scientists to study and diagnose environmental problems, utilising the evidence in lawsuits, petitions to government and public campaigns. One of the most high-profile uses of science in an environmental campaign was deployed by Greenpeace to stop the deep-sea disposal of the Brent Spar oil-storage buoy in the North Sea in 1995.[25]

54 Science and the environment

The Brent Spar was owned by the Shell oil company. Shell had identified deep-sea disposal in UK waters as the best environmental option at reasonable cost. Its decision was supported by technical studies and by the UK government. Greenpeace had a long-standing opposition to deep-sea dumping and quickly acted to occupy the buoy before it was towed to its dumping site. As with many Greenpeace campaigns (see Chapter 2), the occupation secured dramatic and widespread media coverage and lasted several weeks. The imagery provided the spark for a Europe-wide boycott of Shell, and during the occupation members of Greenpeace also assessed the toxic material on the buoy. Shortly afterwards they announced that the Brent Spar still contained thousands of tonnes of waste oil, a finding that directly challenged the positions of Shell and the UK government that the platform was almost empty of oil and that this was the best environmental option. With no third-party observers, the debate over the future of the Brent Spar centred on public trust of an environmental campaign group, a multinational corporation and a government ministry. This placed Greenpeace on the front foot – it was a trusted brand, it had no ulterior motive, and the films and images it provided dominated the news agenda. Shell was forced to shelve its preferred disposal option and take stock of the situation. However, a couple of months later it emerged that Greenpeace had made a mistake: it had sampled oil from the wrong part of the buoy and produced a false measurement. When Greenpeace admitted its mistake it was criticised by the British government and the media. What seemed like a successful campaign became an exercise in damage limitation, with trust in the Greenpeace brand diminishing among the media and the British public. Although the false measurement was a mistake rather than an exaggeration of the facts, trust in the environmental movement as a whole was damaged. Those who are inclined to be sceptical of environmental arguments tend to be more so when they know environmentalists have been wrong in the past. This lesson applies to any institution whose reputation is damaged by the misuse of science, including, and perhaps especially, scientific institutions themselves. In recent years this issue has come to the fore in the shape of attacks on scientists on both sides of the climate change debate.

When the IPCC was created, its purpose was to make climate science relevant, understandable and clear. The process of developing IPCC reports was carefully designed to create ownership by the scientific community and by world governments, who agreed report conclusions sentence by sentence. Despite, or perhaps because of, this carefully produced consensus, each of the IPCC reports has been challenged.

For much of the 1990s, the Global Climate Coalition, an American industrial grouping formed shortly after the IPCC, challenged the levels of scientific certainty set out in IPCC publications. In 1995 the *Wall Street Journal* picked up and published claims that editorial changes to the second report on the science of climate change were in violation of IPCC rules of procedure and would 'deceive policy makers and the public into believing that the scientific evidence shows human activities are causing global warming'.[26] These were strongly refuted by forty lead authors and contributors to the IPCC Working Group. They linked the story to 'similar claims of procedural improprieties' made by the Global Climate Coalition that 'conjure visions of sinister conspiracies that are entirely unfounded'.[27] Disputes like this between scientists and industrial interests were often conducted through the media and third-party commentators, as in the *Wall Street Journal* case. Challenges to the scientific consensus of the IPCC were more controversial and newsworthy than statements supporting their work and so garnered wide attention. Academics such as the American physicist Fred Singer (b. 1924) and the Danish statistician Bjørn Lomborg (b. 1965) added scientific authority to a continuous stream of challenges to climate science. Direct conflict broke out in 2006 when Exxon Mobil, the world's richest company and a member of the Global Climate Coalition, was challenged in an exchange of letters that became public with the Royal Society, the world's oldest scientific academy.[28] This move came shortly before the fourth IPCC report concluded that there was a 90 per cent chance that anthropocentric greenhouse gas emissions caused most of the observed increase in global temperatures since the mid-twentieth century (see Chapter 3), but by this time questions over the certainty of evidence for climate change were firmly established in the public consciousness.

The challenge to climate science reached a new peak after approximately 1000 emails from the Climatic Research Unit (CRU) at the University of East Anglia (UEA) were hacked and posted on the internet in November 2009. CRU specialises in working on the development of global temperature trends and its work plays an important role in climate science, though it is not the only research group to have developed temperature records. As the profile of climate change science increased, the work of CRU, like many other research institutes, came under greater scrutiny and was challenged by other scientists and interested parties. The most controversial of the released emails from CRU dealt with the rejection of data requests from climate sceptics, and apparent manipulation of the IPCC peer-review process to exclude sceptical research. The emails were quickly picked up by the world's media and by prominent climate sceptics, and shook public and political confidence in climate science and the IPCC. This was a public relations disaster from which climate science is still recovering, its seriousness reflected by the fact that three independent reviews were commissioned: two by UEA into the science undertaken by CRU and the conduct of scientists involved, and one by the British government. A fourth review was launched into the IPCC a few months later, following exposure of a mistake in the fourth assessment regarding glacial melt. Each review cleared the CRU scientists involved of the allegations against them. The Muir Russell emails review found 'their rigour and honesty as scientists are not in doubt' and that it 'did not find any evidence of behaviour that might undermine the conclusions of the IPCC assessments'. However, it also concluded that they had displayed a 'consistent pattern of failing to display the proper degree of openness'.[29] This led to further challenges to the scientific authority on climate change. In the UK and USA, internet blogs and comment boards, together with newspaper and television commentaries, challenged peer-reviewed publications, the IPCC process and individual scientists' reputations. the *Daily Telegraph*, the most widely circulated broadsheet in the UK, summarised the atmosphere of hostility, claiming nobody was listening to scientists any more and describing them as 'white-coated prima donnas and narcissists [...] pointy heads in lab coats [who] have reassumed the role of mad cranks'.[30]

How the science of climate change can be communicated to a public audience without being misinterpreted or biased by political arguments is one of the major dilemmas facing the IPCC today. It has a long-standing rule that its only outputs will be official reports which the media translate themselves. This should have protected the science and the scientists from controversy, but has failed to do so. Meanwhile, the absence of IPCC lead authors explaining their findings under IPCC auspices through popular media has diluted the voice of scientists in the public debate. Changing this rule will not necessarily solve this issue; when the Royal Society attempted to write a plain English guide to climate change, it was forced to change its wording following complaints by some of its own members. The biologist E. O. Wilson (b. 1929) has observed that 'any new idea will take some serious hits', but that if sound, ideas will ultimately survive.[31] Anthropogenic climate change looks set to be contested for some time, but the problem for those who view climate change science as conclusive is that it is no longer a purely scientific issue. As with the idea of ecology, acid rain and GM food, the issue of climate change is imbued with cultural and political meaning. Securing consensus on this most polarised and vociferously argued of environmental issues goes far beyond the limits of scientific understanding.

Understanding science and the environment

This chapter has examined how science has been used to identify environmental problems and solutions, and in doing so has influenced the formulation of environmental policy and public opinion. Over the past fifty years, science has driven the environmental agenda, explaining the cause and impact of environmental problems and the implications they have for society as a whole. Science has contributed to providing solutions to environmental problems, particularly environmental pollution. Without science, there would be little understanding of acid rain, the short- and long-term health effects of toxic chemicals, depletion of the ozone layer or the implications of climate change. Yet many environmentalists are ambivalent or suspicious of the role of science. This is because science has been central to the research and development of nuclear energy, pesticide use, genetic and nanotechnology and industrial development, which have caused environmental pollution or pose a perceived risk to human health and the environment. For some environmentalists, science is seen as being about the control, rather than protection, of nature.

The climate change debate has challenged the authority of science to provide a definitive conclusion on an environmental issue that could determine the future survival of humankind. The current scepticism surrounding the science of climate change has damaged one of the environment movement's most potent weapons. Scientific analysis can no longer be relied on to settle debates or secure public support for campaigns. Science based on evidence is now viewed as just one of the many different opinions that exist, especially in an age when the internet allows different interest groups to express their opinions and perpetuate their own conspiracy theories to an unsuspecting audience. The challenge for the environmental movement is to rebuild public trust in the way it uses science to support arguments in order to take action to address environmental issues. Environmentalists will need to re-examine their own trust in science and how they use science in future campaigning. This will require communicating stories about how science and technology can be utilised to produce a positive and greener future.

5 Economics and the environment

Over the past half-century, the development of concepts and theories that recognise the economic value of the environment has become increasingly central to the environmental cause. As with scientific evidence, economic analysis shapes the decisions of policy makers. Yet there is no complete theory of economics and the environment, and as a consequence the environment has had little influence on the economics profession.[1] Compared with environmental science, environmental economics is relatively undeveloped. Environmentalists do not subscribe to any particular economic perspective, nor do they have an alternative of their own. Instead, a series of academics have attempted to outline environmental constraints to the economic system and to move away from the focus on economic growth. Others have developed ways of ensuring environmental interests are reflected in the market economy. Controversially, this has led to the treatment of environmental resources as privately rather than publicly owned commodities. Meanwhile, the ongoing global economic crisis has provided real opportunities for environmentalists to promote a greener economic system.

Early economic thought

Classical economic theory has always recognised natural resources, or more specifically the use of land, as one of the foundations of national wealth. In *The Wealth of Nations* Adam Smith (1723–90) described rent from the use of land, the wages of labour and profits of stock as 'the three original sources of all revenue as well as of all exchangeable value. All other revenue is ultimately derived from some one or other of these.'[2] He also singled out rent derived from the use of land as a source of revenue 'more stable and permanent' than interest from money or profits from stock; accordingly he described it as 'the principal source of the public revenue of many a great nation'.[3] As countries industrialised, the role of land as a factor of production was lost and the focus of economic theory moved to wage labour and capital stock as political economists David Ricardo (1772–1823) and, later, Karl Marx (1818–83) set out their work on economics. As a consequence, land economics, or economics of the environment, did not develop fully into a field of its own until the emergence of contemporary environmentalism.

Where eighteenth- and nineteenth-century economists turned their attention to land, it was to emphasise the value of the services it provided through the provision of raw materials and food. Karl Marx described land as providing a 'reservoir' of resources for coal and minerals, as 'powers of nature' driving mills, and as the 'element of production' for agriculture.[4] Availability of land and, implicitly, food was a particular concern of early classical economists. Anne-Robert-Jacques Turgot (1727–81) outlined a law of diminishing returns in agriculture, arguing that there was a maximum point of land productivity that was impossible to surpass. This implied that the amount of available land placed a constraint on population and wealth, an idea forcefully argued by Thomas Malthus (1766–1834) in *An Essay on the Principle of Population, as it Affects the Future Improvement of Society* (1798), Malthus explained that population growth, driven initially by surplus food production, would eventually be constrained by limits to productive land and a resultant shortage of food. As a consequence, he saw society as under permanent threat of starvation unless measures were taken to limit population expansion.

As nations industrialised, economists became concerned about the limits to industrial and agricultural productivity. In 1865, William Stanley Jevons (1835–82) published *The Coal Question: An Inquiry Concerning the Progress of the Nation, and the Probable Exhaustion of our Coal-mines*, in which he argued that improvements in fuel efficiency tended to increase, rather than decrease, fuel use: 'It is a confusion of ideas to suppose that the economical use of fuel is equivalent to diminished consumption. The very contrary is the truth.'[5] Modern concerns about the impacts of population growth and technology on the environment have changed little since Malthus and Jevons.

As interest in productivity increased, John Stuart Mill (1806–73) was among the first economists to treat the environment as more than a unit of land or a means of production. In 1862, he published the *Principles of Political Economy with some of their Applications to Social Philosophy*, in which he championed the 'stationary state economy' and warned against the drive for unlimited economic growth:

> Nor is there much satisfaction in contemplating the world with nothing left to the spontaneous activity of nature; with every rod of land brought into cultivation, which is capable of growing food for human beings; every flowery waste or natural pasture ploughed up, all quadrupeds or birds which are not domesticated for man's use exterminated as rivals for his food, every hedgerow or superfluous tree rooted out, and scarcely a place left where a wild shrub or flower could grow without being eradicated as a weed in the name of improved agriculture.[6]

This passage points to what Mill described as the 'disagreeable symptoms' of industrial progress, which often went unrecognised in economic thought. Later economist Arthur C. Pigou (1877–1959) argued that when the detrimental effects of an activity went unrecognised, then the government should intervene. He described these detrimental effects as negative externalities, and in doing so introduced a concept that is now central to modern environmental economics.[7]

As this brief survey demonstrates, the concept of the environment was not a focus of early economists. However, many of them developed theories that influenced the future of environmental thought and remain at the heart of environmental economics. These theories become more prominent as the drive for economic growth became a dominant feature of the twentieth century.

Economic growth and production

The post-war period saw many nations equating economic growth with progress driven by technological innovation. In 1944, against the backdrop of the Second World War, forty-four countries gathered together at Bretton Woods in the US state of New Hampshire. The aim of the conference was to ensure post-war peace and prosperity through economic cooperation. The meeting led to the establishment of the IMF and the International Bank for Reconstruction and Development (now the World Bank). In the aftermath of the Second World War, the focus of the international community was on creating a stronger economic foundation for the rebuilding of European countries. The US European Recovery Program, also known as the Marshall Plan, ran from 1947 to 1951 and provided aid to repair the devastation of major war areas and begin economic reconstruction. The aim of the Plan was also to prevent the spread of communism in Western Europe and to stabilise the international order to favour the development of political democracy and free-market economies. Meanwhile, the USA experienced an economic boom on the back of increased production and exports during the Second World War.

By the late 1950s, the standard of living of a large proportion of American society was without historical parallel. In *The Affluent Society* (1958), the American economist John Kenneth Galbraith (1908–2006), reflecting on the continued focus on production as a measure of progress, observed:

> More die in the United States of too much food than too little [...] Yet production remains central to our thoughts. There is no tendency to take it, like sun and water, for granted; on the contrary, it continues to measure the quality and progress of our civilisation.[8]

This drive for economic growth raised concerns about resource availability. The rapid growth of the USA meant that it was quickly becoming a net importer of oil and other raw materials. As early as 1951, President Harry S. Truman (1884–1972) established a presidential commission to examine the future supply of minerals, energy and agricultural resources. The following year the Paley Commission, chaired by William Paley (1901–90), produced a five-volume report: *Resources for Freedom: Foundations for Growth and Security*. The study revealed that there had been an unprecedented increase in natural resource usage since the First World War, and highlighted the importance of natural resources to the development of the US economy.[9]

Whereas the Paley Report argued for a measured approach to resource planning, a number of controversial doomsday prophecies had already been published. In the Malthusian tradition, many of these books focused on overpopulation. These included Henry Fairfield Osborn Jr's (1887–1969) *Our Plundered Planet* and William Vogt's (1902–68) *Road to Survival*, both published in 1948.[10] Over a decade later, David Brower (1912–2000), Executive Director of the Sierra Club, suggested to biologist Paul R. Ehrlich (b. 1932) that he summarise in book form the argument that the population issue should be addressed by the environmental movement. Ehrlich published *The Population Bomb* in 1968, and directly linked population growth to the Earth's capacity to sustain humankind.[11] By this time, the world was experiencing the highest rate of population growth recorded and looked set to add an extra billion people every fifteen years. Concern over the rate of population growth was already reaching high levels when, in 1969, US President Richard Nixon (1913–94) gave a special message to Congress on 'the problems of population growth'.

While many people were concerned with population growth, others challenged the idea of unlimited economic growth. In his 1966 essay 'The Economics of the Coming Spaceship Earth',[12] Kenneth E. Boulding (1910–93) challenged neoclassical economic ideas of an 'open' economic system without finite resources and a limited assimilative capacity to absorb waste. He called the open economy a 'cowboy' economy, symbolic of a cowboy's 'reckless, exploitative, romantic and violent behaviour'. He saw the closed economy of the future as a 'spaceman' economy, where the Earth is a single spaceship with limited reservoirs of resources and capacity to deal with pollution.[13]

Ehrlich and Barry Commoner (b. 1917) became two of the most prominent critics of the focus on economic growth as a measure of progress. Although they did not always agree on how to explain the relationship between human activity and the environment, their debates encapsulated the core environmental arguments against growth. In a critique of Commoner's book *The Closing Circle* (1971), Ehrlich and his colleague John P. Holdren (b. 1944) accused Commoner of placing too great an emphasis on 'faulty technology' and of underplaying the role of population and affluence. At the same time, they rewrote and simplified an equation he had used to show that environmental impacts were driven by multiple interrelated factors. The IPAT equation explained how environmental impacts (I) are a factor of three major determinants: population (P), affluence (A) and technology (T): $I = P \times A \times T$. This simple mathematical concept brought together Ehrlich, Commoner and Holdren's concerns about the prevailing focus on economic growth.[14]

For a time it became fashionable to challenge the use of productivity indicators as the predominant measure of national progress. In March 1968, Robert F. Kennedy (1925–68) delivered a campaign speech at the University of Kansas where he explained the shortcomings of using gross national product (GNP) to measure progress:

> Too much and for too long, we seemed to have surrendered personal excellence and community values in the mere accumulation of material things. Our gross national product […] counts air pollution and cigarette advertising […] it counts the destruction of the redwood and the loss of our natural wonder in chaotic sprawl. Yet the gross national product does not allow for the health of our children […] the intelligence of our public debate or the integrity of our public officials. It measures neither our wit nor our courage, neither our wisdom nor our learning, neither our compassion nor

our devotion to our country, it measures everything in short, except that which makes life worthwhile.[15]

Beyond this high political rhetoric, politicians did little to challenge the idea of economic growth. Many of the arguments against economic growth originated in the academic sphere and were publicised by individuals and groups concerned about the future of society and the environment. In 1968, the industrialist Aurelio Peccei (1908–84) and Scottish scientist Alexander King (1909–2007) invited an international group of professionals from industry, academia and civil society to a villa in Rome. The group discussed international affairs and a shared concern with resource consumption. Following the meeting, the participants established the Club of Rome as a focal point for their shared concerns. The Club's first report, *The Limits to Growth* (1972), was underpinned by the work of a group of systems scientists at the Massachusetts Institute of Technology (MIT), who had developed the first integrated global model linking the world economy and the environment.[16] The study examined the interactions of five subsystems of the global economic system: population, food production, industrial production, pollution, and consumption of non-renewable natural resources.[17] Based on the scenarios produced by the model, the report concluded:

> If the present growth trends in world population, industrialization, pollution, food production, and resource depletion continue unchanged, the limits to growth on this planet will be reached sometime within the next one hundred years. The most probable result will be a rather sudden and uncontrollable decline in both population and industrial capacity.[18]

The Limits to Growth received widespread global attention and highlighted the potential for economic models to trace the interconnections and feedback between various sectors and trends. But, once published, these scenarios became the target of counter-arguments from other academics and commentators. Julian Simon (1932–98) was among the most prominent academics to challenge the idea that there are physical limits to resources that must ultimately constrain economic growth. His arguments were summarised in *The Ultimate Resource* (1981). Simon also entered a wager with Ehrlich regarding the prices of five metals. Ehrlich predicted prices of each metal would rise between 1980 and 1990, demonstrating their growing scarcity. Simon predicted they would fall as technology and substitution would keep prices low. Simon won the bet, though Ehrlich insisted that prices would eventually rise in the longer term. Others have argued that prices are not an appropriate indicator to settle this debate as they are suitable only for illustrating the relative scarcity of resources, rather than their absolute scarcity.[19]

The birth of ecological economics

Boulding's use of the spaceship Earth metaphor made the resource limitations of the economic system understandable to the wider public. At much the same time, the mathematical economist Nicholas Georgescu-Roegen (1906–94) applied similar ideas to economic theory. In *The Entropy Law and the Economic Process* (1971), Georgescu-Roegen explained that whenever energy is used, the amount of usable energy available to society declines. This argument is based on the second law of thermodynamics, which states that although energy cannot be created or destroyed, it can be dispersed in less usable forms. Industrial activity disperses energy by transforming available but limited energy sources (such as fossil fuels) into waste. Accordingly, the amount of easily available fuel is continuously dwindling away; eventually the limited stock of fossil fuels on which modern society is dependent will have to be substituted by other sources of energy such as solar power. These ideas resulted in Georgescu-Roegen coming to conclusions about resource availability and the role of technology that were very different from those of other academics. As Herman E. Daly (b. 1938) later observed, Georgescu-Roegen predicted that the need for biofuels would place land for energy crops in competition with land for food 'when most economists were talking about feeding the world with petroleum'.[20]

Georgescu-Roegen went on to dedicate his academic career to developing what he called a bioeconomic programme.[21] This emphasised the importance of viable technologies that could maintain economic activity over the long term without using irreplaceable resources. This argument was shared by Ernst F. Schumacher (1911–77), who championed the use of appropriate technology in *Small is Beautiful: A Study of Economics as if People Mattered* (1973). Like Georgescu-Roegen, Schumacher argued that natural resources should be treated as capital, not expandable income. By utilising resources on an industrial scale, and at an unprecedented speed, society was mining its natural capital rather than living off its dividend. What was needed instead was an ecologically efficient distribution of resources that maximised human wellbeing over time with the aim of obtaining the maximum amount of wellbeing with the minimum amount of consumption.

Combined together, the works of Boulding, Georgescu-Roegen and Schumacher provided the foundation for modern-day ecological economics. Daly and Robert Costanza (b. 1950) further developed the ideas of their predecessors in ecological economics. Daly is most strongly associated with his attempt to articulate an alternative approach to the conventional growth paradigm in the form of the steady-state economy (SSE). This takes as its starting point the idea that traditional growth has expanded the economy to a size that must now conform to global environmental constraints. Further economic growth will be uneconomic because it will produce more social and environmental costs than it does benefits. Therefore an SSE is needed: 'following [John Stewart] Mill we might define a SSE as an economy with constant population and constant stock of capital, maintained by a low rate of throughput that is within the regenerative and assimilative capacities of the ecosystem'.[22] Daly argues that this is a system that supports qualitative development but not quantitative growth; it produces better outcomes, not more outputs. This shift in focus is still not widely reflected in mainstream economic thinking but it has had an impact on the way policy makers think about measuring progress in society.

In the 1980s, the need to provide alternatives to the gross domestic product (GDP) was highlighted by feminist economist Marilyn Waring (b. 1952), who criticised the GDP as a system which 'counts oil spills and wars as contributors to economic growth, while child-rearing and housekeeping are deemed valueless'.[23] Following this, Daly and John B. Cobb (b. 1925) constructed an index of sustainable economic welfare intended to replace GNP as a measure of economic wellbeing. According to this index, Americans' economic wellbeing increased substantially during the 1950s and 1960s, levelled off from 1968 until the end of the 1970s, and declined after 1980.[24] Since then a number of alternative measures to economic progress have been developed, many linked to the idea of sustainable development. Measures such as the ecological footprint, genuine progress indicator and happy planet index have been applied to national economies, but none has supplanted economic measures as the primary measure of a country's progress. In 2010 the World Bank launched a plan, backed by India, Mexico and a number of other countries, to create an accounting measure that puts the natural wealth of nations alongside financial measurements such as GDP. Developing ways to calculate the economic value of nature is a rapidly developing aspect of environmental economics.[25]

Valuing nature

Ecological economics is as much about ensuring the environment is recognised in standard economic theory as setting out an alternative to a capitalist (or communist) economic system. By attributing a monetary value to the environment and demonstrating the cost of its destruction, some economists have sought to reflect its value to society. An early attempt at costing the damage caused by air pollution was made by the Beaver Committee in the mid-1950s (see Chapter 4). In making the case for action to tackle air pollution, they estimated that the total economic loss of damage to infrastructure, buildings and even laundry, together with the loss of economic efficiency related to this damage, ran to hundreds of millions of pounds.[26]

Cost–benefit analysis has been widely used to make the case for environmental protection and to choose between different environmental protection options. Agencies responsible for environmental regulations such as the EPA in the USA have used cost–benefit analysis extensively, but its application can be complex and controversial and is not always trusted by environmental campaigners or regulated industries. When the Roskill Commission proposed a location for a third runway in London in the early 1970s, it used social cost–benefit analysis to support its case. One of the most important issues to consider was noise pollution, but its application of cost measures to noise was widely challenged. This early application of cost–benefit analysis highlighted the difficulty of recognising the multiple public values of the environment in economic terms. Georgescu-Roegen was among those who challenged this emphasis on using economic methods to solve environmental policy questions:

> Only economists still put the cart before the horse by claiming that the growing turmoil of mankind can be eliminated if prices are right. The truth is that only if our values are right will prices also be so.[27]

Of course, people have recognised the multiple values of the environment for centuries. An approach to communicating this in a structured way has its origins in the 1970s, when the functioning of ecosystems was related to the provision of services. An 1970 MIT report of the Study of Critical Environmental Problems, entitled *Man's Impact on the Global Environment: Assessment and Recommendations for Action*, described nine 'environmental services' that would decline if the functioning of ecosystems were damaged. Holdren and Ehrlich advocated this idea and in an article for *American Scientist* described the 'public service functions of the environment'.[28] Throughout the 1980s and 1990s, the idea was developed further, applied to biodiversity assessments, and then used as a central organising concept for the Millennium

Ecosystem Assessment, undertaken between 2001 and 2005. The Millennium Ecosystem Assessment examined the consequences of ecosystem change on human wellbeing, and provided a global overview of conditions of the world's ecosystems and the services they provide to humanity. It defined the four categories of ecosystem services that contribute to human wellbeing as: provisioning services, such as food; regulating services, such as filtration of pollutants and flood control; cultural services, such as recreation; and supporting services, such as soil formation and photosynthesis.[29]

The power of the ecosystem services approach is that it provides a way for economists to translate ecological functions such as pollination and climate regulation into a language that makes clear their human utility and value. It reinstates the economic significance of the environment as a provider of the basic material for a good life, supporting health and good social relations, providing security, and creating the conditions for freedom of choice and action. This is attractive conceptually, but it does not overcome the problem of establishing a market price that reflects services that are not traded in the market. The allocation of a price to ecosystems services is challenging. However, in the late 1980s Robert Costanza and colleagues attempted to estimate the value of ecosystem services provided by the Earth's biosphere. They estimated the value of the services provided by the ecosystem to humanity at between US$16–54 trillion per year. The majority of these services are still outside the market economy.[30]

One of the great challenges for contemporary ecological economists is ensuring the value of the environment is captured through market signals that tax environmental 'bads' and support environmental 'goods'. Because many ecosystem services are not recognised in the market system, the full cost of their degradation is not considered. Following Pigou, these negative externalities should be regarded as market failures and corrected. This is an argument that has been applied to a wide range of environmental policies from waste management to climate change.

In his review of the economics of climate change, Sir Nicholas Stern (b. 1946) described climate change as 'market failure on the greatest scale the world has seen'.[31] The 2006 Stern Review is the most high-profile example of economic theory presenting the case for environmental action. Just as the science of climate change has been subject to intense public discussion, Stern's estimate that the overall cost of not taking action would be higher than the cost of taking action stimulated international debate. At the heart of this debate is the valuation of the future; economic analysis typically applies discount rates to values in future years to make them directly comparable with present values. Low discount rates make the future more important, high discount rates make it less so.[32] Stern used a near-zero discount rate to underpin his argument; this was an ethically driven decision that reflected the long-term impact of climate change on future generations. Some economists, such as William Nordhaus (b. 1941), use much higher discount rates that lead them to conclude that Stern's approach is inefficient because early action is more expensive than necessary.[33] The varying conclusions that the application of different discount rates can bring mean that 'it is not an exaggeration to say that the discount rate is the most important single number in climate economics'.[34] As an alternative approach, some economists argue that climate change policy should be treated as insurance against worst-case scenarios rather than a measure that can be subjected to cost–benefit analysis.

Although the debate regarding the economics of climate change continues, governments have acted to establish a price for carbon. The EU has established an emissions trading scheme, and the Kyoto Protocol allows for the purchase of emissions-reduction credits through the Clean Development Mechanism. The role of forests in the carbon cycle and their rate of destruction mean that international forest financing could also reduce global carbon emissions, benefit developing countries and help preserve forest ecosystems.[35] Business has much to gain from the pricing of ecosystem services, but it also has potentially enormous environmental liabilities. In 2010, a UNEP report estimated that 3000 listed companies were responsible for US$2.15 trillion worth of environmental damage in 2008, equivalent to 7 per cent off their combined revenues. Greenhouse gas emissions accounted for approximately 70 per cent of the total of those externalities valued.[36] The costs incurred by the global oil and gas company BP in cleaning up the 2010 *Deepwater Horizon* oil spill in the Gulf of Mexico illustrate the real-world economic impact of ecological liabilities. In many parts of the world, multinational companies are fighting cases to avoid incurring liabilities for pollution that run to many billions of dollars. In recognition of these issues, some business sectors are exploring 'no net loss' or 'net positive impact' initiatives in which their impacts are offset by undertaking environmental activities of at least equal value.[37]

Privatising common resources

The monetary valuation of ecosystem services does not imply that they need to be privatised and traded on the market. Environmentalists are split on this topic, with some viewing the environment as a common resource free to all, others arguing that the problem with a resource that is free to all is that it tends to be over-used by society. In 1967, Garrett Hardin (1915–2003) developed the notion of the 'tragedy of the commons' where he used the analogy of common grazing land to illustrate that sharing common resources leads to over-use. Each herdsman as a rational individual seeks to maximise his gain. By adding one more animal to the common land, the herdsman will gain benefits while the overgrazing caused by the additional animal will have a detrimental effect on other herdsmen who use the land. The rational herdsman concludes that he would benefit from adding another animal to the common land. If this is the conclusion of all the herdsmen, it will ultimately lead to the 'tragedy' as each herdsman is locked into a system that compels him to increase his herd without limit. Hardin uses the tragedy of the commons to explain the problem of pollution, which results in polluting emissions entering the natural environment. The polluter as a rational man will come to the same conclusion as the herdsmen, that the cost of polluting can be less than the treatment or abatement of polluting emissions. Hardin concludes that 'Freedom on the commons brings ruin to all' and that 'we are locked into a system of "fouling our own nest" so long as we behave as independent rational, free-enterprises'. His solution was 'mutual coercion mutually agreed upon'.[38]

Hardin's ideas have been used to support the privatisation of commonly owned resources. However, the debate over privatisation is strongly contested, and links environmental issues to those of community empowerment and international development. The idea of privatisation of natural resources has proved particularly controversial in relation to water usage. In 1992, the International Conference on Water and the Environment agreed that 'water has an economic value in all its competing uses and should be recognised as an economic good'.[39] This is in line with the ecosystem services approach and supports the pricing of water resources so as to incentivise careful use in the developed and developing worlds. In the developing world, where per capita incomes are low, this idea can be controversial because low-income groups may find they are priced out of purchasing clean water. Civil society groups have argued that 'access to basic water and sanitation are universal rights, and cannot therefore by negotiated as commodities'.[40] But, given the condition of many public sector water management organisations in the developing world, the World Bank and others have supported a move towards large-scale private sector water resource management. This has not always been met with support among poor communities. When a privately run water company increased the price of water and sanitation in the Bolivian town of Cochabamba, this set in motion a chain of protests against privatisation and a political upheaval that swept the indigenous people's leader Evo Morales (b. 1959) to electoral victory in 2003.

Recently, Hardin's analogy has been criticised because it ignores the powerful sense of community obligation that could exist and act as a deterrent for abuse of common resources. The Nobel Prize-winning economist Elinor Ostrom (b. 1933) has argued that Hardin's work has been used to rationalise central government control of all common pool resources such as fisheries, groundwater basins and irrigation systems, and to paint a disempowering and pessimistic picture of the human prospect.[41] According to Ostrom, an approach to resolving the problem of the commons is the design of durable, cooperative institutions that are organised and governed by the resource users themselves.[42]

A Global Green New Deal

Just as environmentalists have challenged economic concepts and measures of progress, they have targeted weak points in the global economic system to argue for a redirection of economic thinking and practice. In 2008, the world experienced multiple crises with regard to fuel, food and finance. The result was the worst international economic recession since the 1930s Great Depression. The 2008–09 global financial crisis led to global per capita income contracting and the volume of world trade declining.[43] For environmentalists, it also provided a unique opportunity to campaign for the international community to develop an economic recovery package that contributed explicitly to environmental objectives.

US President Franklin D. Roosevelt's (1882–1945) response to the 1929 Great Depression was a series of economic programmes called the New Deal, which focused on relief, recovery and reform. Following in his footsteps, UNEP instigated the Global Green New Deal (GGND) initiative in December 2008. The GGND included an economic stimulus package aimed at reviving the global economy recovery, creating jobs, reducing carbon dependency and environmental degradation, and ending extreme world poverty by 2015. The GGND aimed to contribute to multilateral and national efforts to address the social, economic and environmental impacts of the financial crisis while simultaneously addressing the interconnected challenges of climate change, food, fuel and water.[44] It recommended that the world's richest economies should spend 1 per cent of global GDP on environmental initiatives over the coming years, and make policy changes at global and national levels to support green fiscal spending. Accordingly GGND gives priority to spending on energy efficiency, sustainable transport, renewable energy, agricultural productivity, freshwater management and sanitation.

The initial response of world leaders to the GGND was positive. In April 2009, UK's then Labour Prime Minister Gordon Brown (b. 1951) held the G20 London Summit to discuss the international response to the financial crisis.[45] A G20 communiqué from the meeting stated 'We will make the transition towards clean, innovative, resource efficient, low carbon technologies and infrastructure [...] We will identify and work together on further measures to build sustainable economies.'[46] At the September 2009 Pittsburgh Summit, the G20 further pledged to enhance global climate change initiatives, improve energy security and phase out fossil fuel subsidies as well as reduce the vulnerability of the world's poor.[47]

In 2009, some G20 governments adopted policies to boost aggregate demand and growth, which included a sizeable green fiscal component. The UK devoted approximately 11 per cent of its US$3.9 billion fiscal stimulus to green investments as well as launching a 'Green economy' budget in April 2009, which included a range of low-carbon investments aimed at creating 400,000 new jobs over an eight-year period. In February 2009, the USA adopted a US$78.5 billion American Recovery and Reinvestment Act, which included measures to retrofit buildings and expand mass transit, freight rail and renewable energy as well as construct a 'smart' electrical grid transmission system.[48]

During the recession, members of the G20 spent over US$520 billion on a green stimulus. The stimulus comprised 16 per cent of all fiscal spending and 0.7 per cent of the G20 GDP, falling short of the 1 per cent GGND recommendation. Only China (3 per cent) and South Korea (5 per cent) devoted a sizeable proportion of fiscal spending to a green stimulus, followed by the EU (0.9 per cent) and the USA (0.9 per cent).[49] China and South Korea used their green stimulus investment as a long-term commitment, ensuring they are better placed to be competitive in the clean technology market and to reduce their national deficits and dependency on foreign oil.

This is the first time there has been a concerted global effort to combine environmental and economic measures to create a low-carbon, resource-efficient and less fossil fuel-dependent economy. However, environmentalists regard the measures taken so far as falling short of the first industrial revolution or New Deal in scope and ambition. Edward B. Barbier, a consultant on the GGND, has argued that the G20 failed to instigate a worldwide green recovery, and called for

72 *Economics and the environment*

further measures to reduce market distortions such as the fossil fuel subsidies and develop effective environmental pricing policies and regulations.

In February 2011, UNEP published *Towards a Green Economy: Pathways to Sustainable Development and Poverty Eradication*, which further advocated green investment on a global scale.[50] The report was part of UNEP's initiative to accelerate sustainable development as a contribution to preparations for the 2012 Rio+20 conference in Brazil. It argued that a green economy was important in developed economies, and could also be a catalyst for growth and poverty eradication in developing countries, where in some cases close to 90 per cent of the GDP of the poor is linked to nature or natural capital such as forests and freshwaters.

To kick-start a transition towards a low-carbon, resource-efficient economy, the report recommended prioritising government spending that stimulates green economic sectors, and limiting spending on environmentally perverse subsidies that damage the environment. Pavan Sukhdev, head of UNEP's green economy work, described existing economic measures, such as the US$600 billion a year spent on global fossil fuel subsidies, as a 'gross misallocation of capital'. As an alternative, the report made a case for investing 2 per cent of global GDP (approximately US$1.3 trillion) a year in green investments across ten key sectors (agriculture, buildings, energy supply, fisheries, forestry, industry including energy efficiency, tourism, transport, waste management and water).

These are persuasive ideas that may become economic orthodoxy in their own right. A key test of their acceptance will be in the actions of multinational institutions such as the World Bank, and the economic decisions of governments. Leading global economies such as Brazil and China are already investing heavily in the green energy sector. There is a growing view that links between the green economy and poverty reduction will become increasingly important as the international community turns its attention to Rio+20.

Understanding economics and the environment

This chapter has examined how ecological economics has developed as a discipline that is critical of standard economic theories while at the same time making use of them. The pursuit of economic growth and prosperity has been at the heart of economics and contemporary capitalism. A core environmental critique of this post-war quest for economic growth is that it has failed to reconcile the objectives of human development, poverty reduction and environmental sustainability. At the same time, environmentalists are encouraged to use economic methods to promote environmental causes and demonstrate their value to the economy. These two approaches do not sit comfortably together.

Many environmentalists regard the relentless pursuit of economic growth as endangering the long-term survival of the human species.[51] As an alternative, they argue for a system where policies are designed explicitly to achieve social and environmental goals, and where growth is a by-product.[52] In response, attempts have been made at 'decoupling' or breaking the link between economic growth and worsening environmental quality.[53] Theoretically this could be achieved by reconfiguring production processes and redesigning goods and services. In doing so, it is hoped that the economy can continue to grow without exceeding ecological limits. Decoupling may lead to increased resource efficiency, use of renewable energy and reduction in material output. However, critics have argued that decoupling has become the acceptable face of sustainability, and that it is a myth to suggest that growth can continue without the need for a fundamental restructuring of economic and social systems.

In *Prosperity Without Growth* (2009), Tim Jackson argues that a different kind of economy is essential for a different kind of prosperity – one where human beings can flourish within the ecological limits of a finite planet. He argues that the growth economy is driven by the consumption and production of novelty, which locks society into an iron cage of consumerism. Change at the personal and societal level is necessary to make the transition to a new form of prosperity that does not depend on unrelenting growth. The structure of the market economy needs to be confronted if real environmental gains are to be achieved. There is a need for a fundamental change to the structure of society – a change on the scale achieved in the industrial revolution but driven by clean, efficient and sustainable renewable energy technologies.

All this requires establishing the ecological boundaries for human activity, abandoning growth economics and transforming the mass consumer culture. But in truth there is no detailed economic treatise that sets out how this model would work in the global economy. Environmentalism is not linked to a mature, convincing political economy that rivals Marxism or challenges the classical liberal theory of Smith and Ricardo. In the absence of a comprehensive theory, environmentalists have promoted fiscal measures, economic valuation and the use of markets in the current economic system with mixed success. These approaches will no doubt become more important, particularly if the scientific argument for environmental action is subject to further criticism.

Ultimately, ecological economics aims to address the interdependence of economies and ecosystems, particularly how these two systems can co-evolve based on principles of sustainable development – equity, intergenerational justice and personal responsibility, and improvement of human wellbeing. The challenge for ecological economists is to translate these principles into hard, convincing economic theory.

6 Popular culture and environment

Widespread public exposure to environmental issues has pushed environmentalism into mainstream western culture to the extent that striving to be 'green' has become a modern-day aspiration. Today people are exposed to green issues from all angles: companies build their brands around environmental claims, governments promote environmental messages, green issues are regularly debated in the media, and people make decisions that express environmental preferences on a regular basis. In this sense it can be said that environmentalism is now part of everyday life. Environmentalism has developed alongside consumerism to become part of contemporary popular culture. The environmental movement will need to address the values, attitudes and behaviours that underpin western consumer culture if a transition to a more sustainable society is to be achieved.

The post-war consumer boom

The introduction of rationing during the Second World War instilled in the wartime generation an appreciation of the scarcity of resources. In Britain, basic food items such as milk, butter, sugar, eggs, cheese and tea, as well as clothing and petrol, were all subject to rationing. Wartime propaganda campaigns used slogans such as 'Make do and mend', 'Dig for victory', 'Is your journey really necessary?' and 'Grow your own' to promote self-sufficiency and the efficient use of resources. As European countries began to rebuild their economies, the post-war Labour government continued rationing, and it was not until July 1954 that all food rationing in the UK came to an end.

At this time, the USA was already experiencing healthy economic growth fuelled by the expansion in its wartime production. In order to modernise industrial and business practices in war-torn Europe, the US Marshall Plan introduced American economic models to reduce trade barriers and rebuild and create a strong economic foundation. This resulted in an unprecedented growth in prosperity over the following two decades. The phenomenal expansion in production and consumption contributed to a post-war baby boom and the rise of consumerism on both sides of the Atlantic.

A rise in car ownership and newly discovered freedom and personal mobility were features of this new generation. In the USA, trolley buses and cable cars were abandoned and railways dismantled. In the space of one year (1945–46), total US car sales leaped from 69,500 to 2.1 million. By 1950, Americans had embraced the car culture, with new car sales totalling 6.7 million.[1] In the UK, the post-war rise in car ownership led to a rapid growth in traffic on the roads from 2.2 million in the 1930s to more than 9 million in 1964.[2] Motorways were introduced to reduce urban traffic, and the 'motorway age' was born when the Preston by-pass was opened in December 1958, followed in November 1959 by the M1, the first long stretch of inter-urban motorway.

With this increase in car ownership and use came concerns over the social and environmental impact of cars. In 1965, Ralph Nader (b. 1934) published *Unsafe at Any Speed*, which examined the reluctance of the car industry to improve both vehicle pollution and safety. Nader's book directly challenged large corporations and prompted a new type of consumer advocacy. In response to the growth in both the number and visibility of consumer organisations, governments introduced new laws and regulations. Within years, both the US Clean Air Act and the National Traffic and Motor Vehicle Safety Act were established.[3]

The 1950s also saw an increase in commercial advertising. Over the decades advertising methods would become more sophisticated, enticing consumers by turning luxuries into perceived necessities. New consumer goods such as televisions, refrigerators and washing machines were produced. In 1953 many families in the UK bought their first television for the coronation of Queen Elizabeth II. Two years later, the BBC's monopoly of television came to an end when the first independent television station, ITV, went on air. ITV introduced television advertising to a British audience. American households were already used to television advertising. The first US television advertisement, for watchmaker Bulova, had been broadcast twelve years earlier and an industry was already developing around this advertising medium. Television provided a new way for companies to sell their products to a wider audience. Writing in the 1955 *Journal of Retailing*, marketing consultant Victor Lebow acknowledged that television was a 'powerful weapon' for producers.[4] He reflected thinking on consumerism during this period:

> Our enormously productive economy demands that we make consumption our way of life, that we convert the buying and use of goods into rituals, that we seek our spiritual satisfactions, our ego satisfactions, in consumption. The measure of social status, of social acceptance, of prestige, is now to be found in our consumptive patterns. The very meaning and significance of our lives today expressed in consumptive terms. The greater the pressures upon the individual to conform to safe and accepted social standards, the more does he tend to express his aspirations and his individuality in terms of what he wears, drives, eats – his home, his car, his pattern of food serving, his hobbies.

Television, together with radio and the press, contributed to the development of a post-war consumer culture. This stimulated an appetite for the consumption of goods and services as well as international travel, which inevitably had environmental consequences. The economist J. K. Galbraith (1908–2006) eloquently identified the imbalance between the new-found private wealth and its environmental effects in his book *The Affluent Society* (1956). In a famous passage he described an American family taking its 'mauve and cerise, air conditioned, power-steered and power-braked automobile' though a city 'made hideous by litter' and into a countryside 'rendered largely invisible by commercial art' to picnic 'on exquisitely packaged food [...] by a polluted stream [...] amid the decaying stench of refuse'.[5] But Galbraith was not alone in voicing concern about the environment, and people were becoming more aware of it as an issue. Television was starting to raise public awareness of pollution. Coverage of the 1969 oil slick fire on the Cuyahoga River and the Santa Barbara Channel oil spill were key moments in the growing media coverage of the human impact on the environment.[6]

From Earthrise to Earth Day

What had been a dream for many people, and a subject of science fiction stories and feature films, became a reality on 20 July 1969 when the US lunar module *Eagle* successfully landed on the moon's surface. The Apollo 11 moon landing is seen as a demonstration of human ingenuity, a mastery over the natural and physical laws that govern the planet achieved by advanced technology. But the extensive television coverage of humanity's first mission to land on the moon, and the images of planet Earth from space, also helped to bring modern environmental concepts into the mainstream. In particular, the view of the whole of the Earth for the very first time from space transformed people's understanding of our place in the universe.[7]

The first pictures of Earth from space were actually taken by the crew of Apollo 8 eight months earlier, on Christmas Eve in December 1968. After returning from the far side of the moon for the fourth time, one of the crew spotted by chance the view of the Earth. His reaction was captured by the on-board tape recorder for posterity: 'Oh, my God! Look at that picture over there!' he exclaimed. 'Wow, that is pretty!'[8] The first image of Earth rising in the vast darkness of space over a lunar landscape became an iconic picture. Initially in black and white, and then in colour, the image became known as 'Earthrise'. Twenty-four years earlier, British astronomer Sir Fred Hoyle (1915–2001) had predicted that, when spaceflight enabled us to see the whole of Earth from space, the view would change us forever. The images of a desolate and lifeless moon contrasted with the blue and white, fertile Earth and provided a stark reminder of humankind's fragility and seeming insignificance in the vastness of space. This fed a growing environmental belief that the economy and human population could not grow forever when there was only one planet to sustain it.

A year after the moon landing, US senator Gaylord Nelson (1916–2005) proposed the first Earth Day on 22 April 1970. The day was marked by a national environment teach-in led by schools, colleges, universities and community groups. Media coverage included a primetime CBS News Special Report called *Earth Day: A Question of Survival*. An estimated 20 million Americans took part in the Earth Day event, which helped environmental issues to be placed firmly in the public consciousness. This led to newly established environmental groups using television advertisements to promote their campaigns. After Earth Day, US President Richard Nixon (1913–94), in his first State of the Union address, acknowledged a growing public awareness of environmental issues when he stated:[9]

> The great question of the seventies is, shall we surrender to our surroundings, or shall we make our peace with nature and begin to make reparations for the damage we have done to our air, to our land, and to our water?

Taking action

Due to post-war affluence, the wartime ethic of re-using and making do with materials ceased to be an everyday habit. By 1970, the Earth Day campaign was again highlighting the need for individuals and communities to do their bit to protect the environment. Early campaigns focused on unsociable actions such as littering, but also on resource issues such as recycling, energy and water use.

In 1971, Keep America Beautiful (KAB) launched the 'Crying Indian' public announcement campaign, which was to become an iconic symbol of personal environmental responsibility. The TV advert followed a Native American Indian chief wandering America's roadways and rivers, and coming across litter and pollution. As the chief wipes a tear from his eye the accompanying slogan states: 'People start pollution. People can stop it.'[10] This marked the beginning of a new focus on the impact of individual actions on the environment.

KAB was founded in 1953 by a group of US corporate and civic leaders to promote and develop a national cleanliness ethic in response to the growing problem of litter.[11] The purpose of the organisation was to reduce litter through public education and advertising, and in 1956 it produced its first public service announcement on litter prevention. KAB was the first organisation to bring littering to the national attention in the USA, and coined the term 'litterbug', which became a household word.

This early effort to educate consumers may not have been conceived entirely in the environment's interests. States were already gearing up to encourage container recycling, and in 1971 the State of Oregon's landmark Bottle Bill became law in spite of intense lobbying by container and beverage industries. The Oregon bill set out to reduce litter and to conserve resources by requiring a five cent deposit on beer and soft drink containers.[12] In 1974, the State of California proposed a similar bill but KAB publicly opposed it, and a year later launched the Clean Community System as an alternative that placed an emphasis on street cleaning and other litter-control activities.[13] Many perceived the opposition to the state bottle bills as serving the industrial members of KAB rather than the broader environmental community. This was seen as an early form of 'greenwash' – disinformation disseminated by an organisation so as to present an environmentally responsible public image.

By now recycling was becoming an established environmental action that everybody could do. In November 1970, Woodbury, New Jersey was the first US city to begin materials recovery, spearheaded by an environmentally concerned community organisation.[14] In 1973, the Ecology Center, a US action-orientated organisation, launched a recycling demonstration project in Berkeley, California collecting newspapers, which became a model for other municipal recycling programmes.[15] In August 1977, the UK's first bottle bank was sited in the car park of the Tesco supermarket in Barnsley, South Yorkshire. The bottle bank was introduced by Stanley Race, then president of the Glass Manufacturers' Federation, with the aim of convincing local authorities that such schemes could be environmentally friendly and pay for themselves. South Yorkshire County Council went on to set the trend for glass recycling in the UK. Over six months 5000 tonnes of glass was collected. The scheme captured the public imagination and was later extended and adopted by other local authorities.[16] By the 1980s, Germany has made considerable progress with glass and paper recycling. The German Green Party had thousands of elected local councillors who worked to establish kerbside recycling collections. By the end of the 1980s, Germany was recycling approximately 50 per cent of its glass packaging, mainly via public collection bins.[17]

Energy use also became a subject requiring public attention. In 1973, an oil export embargo of the Organization of the Petroleum Exporting Countries (OPEC) by major Arab oil-producing states caused a hike in the price of oil, leading to an oil crisis. In the UK this caused national debates on energy security and led the government to introduce a national 'Save it' campaign to promote energy conservation. A combination of increasing environmental awareness, rising energy costs and power cuts in UK homes contributed to this push for individuals to save energy.

Other notable public information campaigns included the UK government's 'Are you doing your bit?' campaign in the late 1990s, and more recently in the 2000s the 'Act on CO_2' campaign. Heightened awareness of environmental issues has meant that consumers have also turned to the market to express their moral, political and environmental concerns. Whereas government campaigns tended to focus on routine consumption, consumers have also begun to seek to green their lifestyles through conspicuous consumption decisions. This is something companies have been quick to exploit.

The rise of the green consumer

The 1980s saw UK Prime Minister Margaret Thatcher and US President Ronald Reagan introduce policies to deregulate the markets. In the UK, key British industries such as British Gas, British Telecom and British Rail were privatised. The much promoted principle of consumer sovereignty placed an emphasis on individuals taking responsibility for their choices. The idea of 'green consumerism' gave individuals the power to vote with their pocket and make accountable governments and companies that did not live up to expected social and environmental standards. Environmental campaign groups mobilised consumer action to boycott products and services associated with animal testing, factory farming and the arms industry. A number of mainly ethical boycotts had successfully led to Barclays Bank pulling out of South Africa due to international opposition to apartheid; Benetton clothing company stopping animal testing; and Nestlé adopting an international code when marketing baby milk substitutes in the developing world.[18]

By now, green campaign groups were organising environmental and consumer boycotts on an international scale. The discovery of the Antarctic ozone hole in 1985 spurred an international effort to sign the Montreal Protocol to curb the production of CFCs, widely used as refrigerants, aerosols and solvents, which contribute to ozone depletion (see Chapter 4). In 1986, the UK FoE published a pamphlet, *The Aerosol Connection*, detailing a list of aerosols that were CFC-free. This was coupled with a publicity campaign encouraging consumers to find out which aerosols they should be buying. When this approach failed to persuade aerosol manufacturers to take action, FoE planned to boycott all the best-selling CFC-based aerosols. The eight largest aerosol companies took the decision to phase out all CFCs by the end of 1989, three days before the boycott campaign was launched. This was partly due to the fear of consumers turning against all aerosols, not just CFC-based aerosols. The eight companies accounted for 65 per cent of the UK toiletries market and were followed by other companies, including major supermarket groups.[19] The then FoE Director, Jonathon Porritt (b. 1950), reflecting on the power of consumer awareness, wrote:

> Consumer awareness is often a somewhat rudimentary weapon, but the industry accurately read the signs of what was happening. Once the Prince of Wales declared that he had banned all aerosols from his household, they knew they were fighting a losing battle.[20]

In 1988, John Elkington (b. 1949) and Julia Hailes (b. 1961) published *The Green Consumer Guide*, which reflected the growing interest in green consumerism and further encouraged individuals who wanted to use their purchasing power to buy the greenest products. The Guide was the first of its kind to focus on green consumer choices and sold over one million copies, demonstrating there was a growing green consumer market. Green products and services were now beginning to span the entire market, and in 1987 a boom in ethical investment saw the launch of six new British ethical funds.[21] The late 1980s saw a peak in consumer awareness of environmental issues. A 1989 survey of Americans found that 89 per cent were concerned about the environmental impacts of the products they bought, while 77 per cent were influenced by a company's environmental reputation.[22,23]

A number of well established brand names became targets for organised consumer action. In 1988, the US environmental groups EDF, Earth Action Network and Kids Against Pollution attacked McDonald's, the largest US fast-food chain, for the amount of rubbish it produced. The polystyrene 'clamshells' in which hamburgers were sold became a symbol of the throwaway society.[24] Tactics adopted by campaigners included consumers sending back used McDonald's wrappers to corporate headquarters, and schoolchildren demonstrating outside its shops. The company was subjected to mounting pressure on its non-recyclable waste and in 1990 agreed to move to paper-based packaging.

Many iconic green brands of today grew rapidly during the 1980s. In 1976, Anita Roddick (1942–2007) founded The Body Shop in Brighton, UK to sell natural beauty products. The Body Shop appealed to the environmentally conscious consumer by sponsoring Greenpeace posters and supporting community trade products. In 1986 it created its own window campaign, 'Save the whale', in collaboration with Greenpeace.[25] Other companies raced to catch up to meet the demand for green products, with supermarket chains, disposable nappy manufacturers and car manufacturers all wanting to be seen as environmentally friendly. The number of green products introduced into national markets rose from 60 in 1986 to 810 in 1991, with green products making up a greater share of all new products, increasing from 1.1 per cent in 1986 to 13.4 per cent in 1991. During this period, many manufacturers informed consumers about the environmental credentials of their products and services. This resulted in an increase in print and TV advertising of green products.[26] A 1989 Gallup poll found that 58 per cent of *Fortune* magazine's 500 list of business executives believed their customers would pay more for products with recyclable packaging or components.[27] At the same time, consumers were wary of companies undertaking 'greenwash' campaigns. One 1990 survey indicated that 47 per cent of customers dismissed environmental claims as mere 'gimmickry'.[28]

Differentiation allows brands to stand out, and environmental labelling provides one way of doing this. With a lack of standards, green-minded consumers found it difficult to distinguish between superficially similar products, priced the same but with different origins, component materials and production standards. One way of addressing this was through labelling, and the EU introduced a voluntary Ecolabel scheme in 1992. The Ecolabel was designed to make it easier for consumers to identify and choose green products and to encourage businesses, services and market products to advertise their environmental credentials. Washing machines, paper towels, writing paper, light bulbs and hairsprays were the first products to carry the EU Ecolabel. The label covered the whole life cycle of a product, from the extraction of raw materials through manufacture, distribution, use and disposal. At the beginning of 2010, more than 1000 EU Ecolabel licences had been awarded, with Italy and France having the highest number of Ecolabel holders.[29]

Over the past five years there has been another peak in consumer interest in green products. In 2007, Britain's leading businesses responded to a resurging green trend, with the supermarket chain Tesco announcing it would be labelling 70,000 products with details of its carbon footprint, and that it would cut carbon emissions from its stores by 75 per cent. Marks & Spencer launched a £200 million 'Plan A' programme to make the company carbon neutral by cutting energy consumption and stocking more products from recycled materials. Similar strategies have been developed by companies to market their products in Canada, New Zealand, USA and Europe. However, high street stores and supermarkets still have a long way to go to address the social and environmental impacts of their entire supply chain.

Like many issues, green consumerism has divided environmentalists: some believe it encourages individuals to question which products they consume, rather than whether they should be consuming them at all. They point out that the world's problems are due to a global consuming class, and that the level of consumption is the major problem, regardless of choice. Despite this criticism, green consumerism has become mainstream, and has been promoted and heavily influenced by the mass media, businesses and campaign groups.

Greening the mainstream

The 1966 US broadcast of *The Undersea World of Jacques Cousteau* brought life under the seas to public attention for the very first time. Cousteau (1910–97) was to be followed by UK TV botanist David Bellamy (b. 1933) and naturalist David Attenborough (b. 1926). In 1979, Attenborough produced a highly acclaimed documentary, *Life on Earth*, which told the story of the evolution of life on the planet. The natural world proved the perfect showcase for colour television and at the same time revolutionised viewers' perspectives of the world. Coral reefs, birds of paradise, tigers and gorillas each wowed prime-time television audiences. David Attenborough's television series in particular exploited new technologies such as infrared cameras to showcase the natural environment.

It took some time for personalities who specialised in environmental issues to be joined by celebrities. US actors Paul Newman (1925–2008) and Ali McGraw (b. 1939) took part in the 1970 Earth Day celebration at Union Square in New York City. Folk singer Pete Seeger (b. 1919) was one of a number of artists who performed at a similar event in Washington, DC.[30] However, it was not until the 1980s, with the success of the Live Aid concert on 13 July 1985 which galvanised a host of international artists to raise money to tackle the Ethiopian famine, that environmentalists realised the power of celebrity endorsement.

A number of celebrity-led or -endorsed environmental campaigns followed Live Aid. In 1989, British musician Sting (b. 1951) founded the Rainforest Foundation International with his wife Trudie Styler (b. 1954) and Belgian film-maker Jean-Pierre Dutilleux. The Foundation responded to the request of Kayapo indigenous leader Raoni Metuktire, who joined Sting in an international campaign to support their fight for the right to own their own land in the Brazilian state of Amazonas. In 1993 this resulted in legal recognition and demarcation of an area of more than 27,359 square kilometres.[31]

However, it was not until the 2000s that 'green celebrity' began to emerge with regularity. In May 2006, US *Vanity Fair*, a magazine of popular culture, fashion and politics, reflected popular environmental awareness when it published its 'Green Issue'. The cover featured Hollywood movie stars Julia Roberts (b. 1967) and George Clooney (b. 1961), and politicians Al Gore (b. 1948) and Robert Kennedy Jr (b. 1954), dressed in complementary shades of green. The four celebrities were photographed by American portrait photographer Annie Leibovitz (b. 1949) and posed Hollywood-style in front of a mossy, ivied backdrop. The cover described global warming as a threat graver than terrorism and called for 'A New American Revolution'. The green issue was produced partly as a response to the increased environmental awareness that followed Hurricane Katrina and the destruction of New Orleans, and marked an attempt to use celebrity to sell sustainability to a moderately interested public.[32] But, like any popular trend, this high-profile coverage lasted only until the novelty wore off. Three years later, *Vanity Fair* announced it would abandon its annual green issue, arguing that the environment had become so integral to the news agenda that there was no longer a need for a dedicated issue.[33]

Climate change has had a more permanent effect on culture more generally, and has even become the subject of high-profile films. In

Popular culture and environment 85

2006, former US Democratic Party Vice President Al Gore's long-standing interest in environmental issues led him to produce the Oscar-winning documentary *An Inconvenient Truth*. This followed the 2004 Hollywood science-fiction disaster film *The Day After Tomorrow*. Both, in their own way, depicted the potentially catastrophic effects of climate change. In 2007, US actor Leonardo DiCaprio (b. 1974) produced and narrated the feature film documentary *The 11th Hour* on the state of the natural environment. The film documented problems facing the planet's life systems, including climate change, deforestation, species extinction and depletion of the oceans' habitats. And in 2009 British environmental campaigner Franny Armstrong (b. 1972) produced the film *The Age of Stupid*, which continued the climate change theme. A drama–documentary–animation hybrid, *The Age of Stupid* stars British actor Pete Postlethwaite (1946–2011), who depicted a man living alone in the devastated world of 2055, watching archive footage from the late 2000s and asking 'Why didn't we stop climate change when we had the chance?'.

In today's consumer age, films are often the starting point for sales of other products. Following on the success of *An Inconvenient Truth*, Gore set out to sell the importance of action on climate change on an epic scale through a global series of Live Earth concerts. The 2007 Live Earth concert called for worldwide action to combat climate change across seven continents, and was broadcast in 132 countries. Described as the 'largest global entertainment event in history', Live Earth staged concerts in New York, London, Sydney, Tokyo, Shanghai, Rio de Janeiro, Johannesburg and Hamburg – as well as special broadcast events in Antarctica, Kyoto and Washington, DC. This monumental music concert featured more than 150 of the world's most popular music acts.

The Age of Stupid's director Franny Armstrong also used her film as a starting point for further campaigning on climate change. In 2008, the Public Interest Research Centre's report *Climate Safety* concluded the need for a 10 per cent reduction in the developed world's emissions by the end of 2010.[34] This inspired Armstrong to found the 10:10 campaign, which encouraged individuals, businesses and organisations to commit to reducing their carbon emissions. The UK-based 10:10 campaign spread across the world, and at the time of writing had campaigns in more than forty countries, including Australia, Ghana, Bangladesh, Russia and Nepal.

The world of fashion has also embraced the environmental cause and lately has contributed to making 'green' fashionable. In 2005, the designer Vivenne Westwood (b. 1941) set up 'Active Resistance' as a project to encourage engagement with humanitarian and environmental issues. Westwood has supported the campaign to combat climate change and invited consumers not to buy new clothes as part of her new eco-philosophy.[35] In 2007, bag designer Anya Hindmarch (b. 1968) designed an unbleached £5 cotton bag with 'I am not a plastic bag' written on it for Sainsbury's supermarket. The bag became so popular it sold out within an hour, contributing to an 'eco-chic' trend in fashion.

Royalty also played a role in promoting environmental issues. HRH Prince Charles, Prince of Wales (b. 1948) has long had an interest in green issues and the natural environment. In the early 1980s, when Prince Charles moved to the Highgrove estate in Gloucestershire, he began the process of converting the Duchy Home Farm, which is part of the estate, to an organic agricultural system. In 1990, he launched his own organic brand, Duchy Originals, which embodies the Prince of Wales's commitment to producing natural, organic products while helping to protect and sustain the countryside and wildlife. In 2007, his household set a target to reduce its carbon emissions by 25 per cent by 2012 against a baseline year of 2007.[36] Following this, in his first speech to the European Parliament on 14 February 2008, the Prince called for EU leadership in the war against climate change. He also used a 2009 BBC lecture to argue that it is essential that people change their behaviour to stop the effects of climate change. The Prince's activities continued in 2010, when he undertook an ecotour of the UK in a bio-fuel-powered Royal Train to promote an initiative to encourage and celebrate sustainable living. The aim of the initiative was to present an inspiring vision of a sustainable future and to assist people across the UK to take practical steps to lead more sustainable lives. At the end of the tour, he held a sustainability festival attended by an estimated 70,000 people and demonstrated how everyone could make a difference.

Together, the movie industry, television, actors, musicians, designers, royalty and other key institutions have all contributed to the popularisation of environmental issues, influencing public attitudes and behaviour. Of course, celebrity culture generally exists to sell goods; climate change articles in magazines sit alongside adverts for luxury cars; serious film documentaries are preceded by commercials; and green lifestyle shops sell luxury items rather than basic essentials. Many environmentalists argue that it is important to recognise that this newfound cultural expression is not the same as environmentally friendly behaviour. Every consumption activity has an impact on the environment – just because a product is green, that does not mean it has no impact at all. This discord between green identity and green action is bound up in people's awareness of, and attitudes to, the environment.

Changing public attitudes

Over the past sixty years, the West has seen a rise in prosperity and material security. Many people have been liberated from the pressure to meet basic material needs (food, shelter and warmth). Consequently, materialistic values have gradually been replaced by 'post-materialistic' values focused on quality of life and spiritual development. Ronald Inglehart (b. 1934) defined this phenomenon as 'post-materialism'. People with post-materialist values are more likely to be receptive to environmental issues.[37] Factors that have influenced the rise of post-material values include increased media coverage of environmental issues and the attention given to the environment in education. It could also be argued that the growth of new occupations in the 1970s and 1980s, such as white-collar public sector jobs, have strengthened and consolidated contemporary environmentalism.[38]

Nonetheless, public awareness of and interest in environmental issues have risen and fallen over the decades. In the USA, public concern for the environment first peaked around the first Earth Day in 1970 and then declined over the following decade. However, by 1980 the US public remained more concerned about environmental quality than in the 1960s.[39] The 1980s saw an increase in environmental concern with the discovery of climate change, the ozone hole and an increase in environmental disasters such as the Union Carbide gas tragedy in India, the Chernobyl nuclear disaster and the Exxon Valdez oil spill. The media, encouraged by campaigners, scientists and policy makers, gave a great deal of coverage to environmental issues during this period. In June 1984, the word 'green' was used 3617 times in selected UK newspapers and magazines; by June 1987 the same publications mentioned 'green' 30,777 times.[40] In 1989, the US *Time* magazine declared 'Endangered Earth' as the 'Planet of the Year' instead of its usual man or woman of the year.[41] US public concern for the environment grew much more quickly than any other issue in the period 1987–90. The environment ranked fourth on a 1990 list of national priorities. Business was blamed for causing much of the environmental pollution, while 78 per cent (up from 56 per cent in 1987) of the public believed 'government needs to make a major effort to solve our environmental problems'.[42]

This general trend in increased coverage and positive attitudes to the environment has continued over the past two decades as different environmental issues have come to the public's attention. New language and terminology have helped maintain the novelty of the environmental cause to the public and the media. In the early 1990s, the term 'low carbon' was rarely used; by 2008 it could be found in over 4000 major world publications.[43] Similarly, the term 'carbon footprint' had become ubiquitous in lifestyle articles and corporate reports by the late 2000s. Particular events have had short-term impacts on media coverage, with environmental issues entering public consciousness on a regular basis. Although it is often suggested that levels of concern for the environment are related to the state of the economy, evidence suggests there is no particular correlation between the environment and other key public concerns. Instead, the environment is a second-order issue, concern for which does not change, but is hidden when other first-order public concerns are raised (such as the economy, immigration and crime). However, evidence suggests there is scope for concern for the environment to shift when there is uncertainty about the issues.

Climate change has become a controversial issue that has divided public opinion. Public understanding of the causes and impacts of climate change and attitudes to the issue have varied within and between countries. The November 2009 'climategate' controversy over climate science (see Chapter 4) contributed to a decline in public concern about climate change, although this was not as significant as some environmentalists feared. A 2010 survey of public attitudes in England revealed that the majority of the public still believed that the climate is changing and were prepared to take action. Most people (71 per cent) remained either fairly or very concerned about climate change, compared with 82 per cent in 2005. Given the 2009 media controversy surrounding climate change science, 40 per cent of respondents thought that the seriousness of climate change has been exaggerated, although 57 per cent believed that most scientists agree that humans are causing climate change.[44]

Although European public attitudes to climate change vary between countries, climate change is still seen as one of the top three most serious problems facing the world. A 2009 EU study found that two-thirds of Europeans felt the climate is a very serious problem. In Turkey, Romania, Bulgaria and Lithuania, citizens felt they were not well informed about the causes and effects of climate change. As a consequence, they were not personally inclined to take action. In contrast, the public of Sweden, Slovenia, UK and Ireland felt well informed about the issue and were willing to take personal action.

There were greater differences of opinion in the Netherlands and UK compared with other European countries. In these countries, more than four in ten citizens thought the seriousness of climate change had been exaggerated and that carbon dioxide emissions have only a marginal impact on global warming. Approximately half the citizens in these two countries classified climate change as a 'very serious problem' – significantly lower than the EU average.[45]

A 2010 Yale University study of US public attitudes to climate change found that 63 per cent of Americans believed that global warming is happening. The study also found gaps in knowledge and common misconceptions about climate change. These misconceptions led some people to doubt that climate change poses a real threat. Only 50 per cent of Americans understood that global warming is caused mostly by human activities. Survey respondents recognised their own limited understanding of the issue. Only one in ten stated that they were 'very well informed' about climate change. Despite 'climategate', the study found that Americans trust scientists and scientific organisations more than any other source of information on climate change. In addition, 75 per cent of respondents said they would like to know more about climate change, and 68 per cent said they would welcome a national programme to teach Americans more about the issue.

This widespread variation in public understanding, knowledge and attitudes to climate change demonstrates that further effort needs to be made by the environmental movement, government and businesses if the mainstream are to be persuaded to change their behaviour and make the transition to low-impact lifestyles.

Changing individual behaviour

The challenges associated with changing individual attitudes and behaviour cannot be underestimated. A large number of socio-economic and cultural factors can shape and constrain an individual's decision to engage in environmentally friendly behaviour. Different groups within society have different values and attitudes, which define both the issues they identify with and their patterns of consumption. Understanding how and why decisions are made and the willingness and potential to change lifestyles is critical to achieving sustained attitudinal and behavioural change. Since almost all aspects of modern western lifestyles contribute to greenhouse gas emissions, it is necessary for the environmental movement to demonstrate that everyone can make a difference, whatever their personal, social or economic circumstances.

The largest environmental impacts of individual consumption are associated with food, energy and personal travel. These activities generate waste and polluting emissions that are a major cause of environmental degradation and contribute to climate change.

Approaches to achieving environmentally friendly behavioural change include top-down mass information and awareness campaigns directed at the whole population. These campaigns aim to 'educate' the public by providing information on environmentally friendly decisions and behaviours. However, such campaigns tend to be intensive, limited in time and expensive. The top-down approach has been criticised for misunderstanding public perceptions of issues. Factors that might influence a decision are often not addressed. These can include, but are not limited to: people's perception of sustainable goods and services as being more expensive; lack of awareness about how to become more sustainable; and mistrust of government bodies, environmental organisations and businesses that promote lifestyle changes.[46]

While some national and local climate change campaigns have succeed in changing individual behaviour, there has not been a significant increase in understanding and engagement. The issue of climate change has always suffered from a perception that its effects are distant in space and time. Equally, campaigns to tackle climate change have sold the threat of what would happen if our current high-impact lifestyles continue unabated. The danger of this 'climate hell' has caused some people to ignore the issue all together.

In the 1940s, US salesman Elmer Wheeler advised businesses on his 'Don't sell the sausage, sell the sizzle!' marketing approach. Wheeler's secret to successful selling was not to advertise the sausage itself, but to focus on the desirable sounds and smells of the 'sizzle'; this is what made people feel hungry and want to buy it. There is increasing recognition that the 'selling the sausage' approach to environmental issues is not delivering the fundamental changes required to stay within ecological limits. A report by the sustainability communications consultancy Futerra, *Sizzle: The New Climate Message*, argues that in order to reinvigorate public and media interest, campaigns need to focus on a vision of a greener life that is positive and appealing to all.[47] New and refined approaches need to be considered to effectively re-engage key groups in society and to win hearts and minds. So far, environmentalists have failed to effectively communicate a compelling vision of a greener future. The challenge of the environmental movement is to communicate a vision that sells a 'green heaven'; one that puts the sizzle back into green behaviour and demonstrates that a transition to a low-carbon society ultimately means a better quality of life for everyone.

Understanding popular culture and the environment

This chapter has examined how environmentalism developed as part of popular culture over the past sixty years. In the 1960s, environmental issues burst into the public consciousness with unprecedented speed and urgency. During these early years, environmentalism had a clear countercultural element, and this has stayed with it over half a century of campaigns, protests and boycotts. The rise of consumerism, influence of the media and emergence of celebrity have all contributed to making environmentalism part of western mainstream culture. It influences practically all aspects of society, to the extent we are now all environmentalists at one level or another.

Despite the increase in environmental awareness, barriers have continued to prevent some individuals from adopting greener lifestyles. The public has tended to engage with local issues rather than distant threats of global environmental destruction. There has been a general reluctance to make changes that are inconvenient or a challenge to established routines. This is due to many individuals being preoccupied with short-term household budgets, especially among low-income households. Evidence suggests that the correlation between green attitudes, knowledge and actual behaviour is often weak, with environmental attitudes being a poor predictor of subsequent behaviour. This inconsistent 'value–action' gap is where attitudes to green behaviour differ from actual behaviour. However, individuals who do not regularly engage in green behaviour may still see themselves as leading a green lifestyle.

This confusion about what a green lifestyle actually entails is evident in the responses to a 2009 UK survey on the issue. A green lifestyle was no longer seen as an alternative lifestyle by half of the respondents, while a quarter of them disagreed that their lifestyle contributed to climate change. The majority of respondents (61 per cent) felt it was worth doing environmentally friendly things, while 55 per cent felt guilty when they do things that harm the planet.[48] From an environmental perspective, all of this is positive, but it suggests that people think they are already living green lifestyles. While there is a willingness to undertake green actions that are easy, such as recycling or switching off lights, there is often a reluctance to change behaviour with regard to car use, long-haul holidays and the purchase of goods. Part of the challenge is that almost every modern-day activity has an environmental impact. A greener lifestyle has to be an easier, convenient and cheaper option for everyone if people are to be encouraged to think about their impact on the planet.

The challenge for the environmental movement is not only to translate awareness into action, but to address the values and beliefs that underpin the mainstream culture of consumerism that defines twenty-first-century living.

7 The future of environmentalism

Since the 1960s, environmentalists have successfully placed the need to protect and manage the environment and natural resources on the political and public agenda. Progress has been made in ensuring the quality of air, water and soil, and in protecting flora and fauna. Environmental organisations have become larger, stronger, better funded and more knowledgeable, and have grown in membership and influence. Yet well financed lobby groups with a vested interest in maintaining the *status quo* have often opposed environmental objectives. In the media, environmentalists are often portrayed as radicals driven by unrealistic ideals rather than sound science. Sometimes environmentalists are too easily described as opposing technological developments that could support societal and environmental progress. Consequently, for each high-profile victory for the environmental movement, there has been a campaign that has stalled or failed. Too often, contemporary environmentalism has tended to be concerned about a separate 'thing' called 'the environment' rather than advancing an alternative worldview that integrates society, economy, ecology and equity.

Climate change is now the greatest challenge for the environmental movement. The urgency to reduce greenhouse gases, the slow progress made in achieving binding international commitments, the controversy over the role of nuclear technology, the style of climate change campaigning and the rise in climate scepticism have all caused fractures within the movement. The failure of the environmental movement to achieve meaningful progress in tackling climate change has led some environmentalists to argue that 'what the environmental movement needs more than anything else right now is a collective step back to rethink everything'.[1] So what does the future hold for environmentalism?

Environmental progress and change

A UN assessment of the state of the global environment, which marked the twentieth anniversary of the Brundtland Commission's *Our Common Future* report, found that while progress has been made in improving the state of the environment, major environmental threats such as climate change, the rate of species extinction and the challenge of feeding a burgeoning population are among the many issues that remain unresolved. In an increasingly globalised, industrialised and interconnected world, human activity continues to drive environmental degradation such as climate change, deforestation, depletion of natural resources and loss of biodiversity.

Globalisation and population growth have been key driving forces of environmental degradation. Globalisation has improved the living standards of many people, but has also increased the global competition for scarce land, water, energy and natural assets. The intensification of strategic resource competition between nation states could lead to increased poverty, state fragility, inflation and economic instability.[2] Forecasts suggest the population of the planet will double to 14 billion by 2100 if no action is taken.[3] However, the impact of population growth must be set alongside the impact of per capita consumption as well as the vast gap between the global consuming class and the global poor. Acknowledging the impact of consumption on the global environment is central to addressing international environmental issues. The task ahead, neatly stated by Ashok Khosla (b. 1940), President of Development Alternatives, 'is to raise the floors, bring down the ceilings and plug the leaks'. In other words, meet the needs of the poor, limit excessive consumption by the rich, and in doing so respect the world's environmental thresholds.[4]

A number of studies have attempted to define environmental thresholds or limits, and to measure the impact of human activity on them. A 2010 WWF analysis of the impact of human activity on the planet found that humanity's ecological footprint has doubled since 1966. In 2007, the footprint exceeded the Earth's biocapacity (the area actually available to produce renewable resources and absorb carbon dioxide) by 50 per cent. According to WWF, it would take 1.5 years for the Earth to produce the resources humanity consumes in a single year. This 'ecological overshoot' is largely attributable to the carbon footprint, which has increased elevenfold since 1961. Carbon emissions in particular, together with food demand, are the major drivers of the escalating footprint.

Further evidence suggests that human pressure on the Earth's ecosystem has reached a point where rapid global environmental change is possible. A seminal paper in *Nature* has developed the notion of planetary boundaries.[5] A total of nine planetary boundaries have been identified: climate change, stratospheric ozone, land-use change, freshwater use, biological diversity, ocean acidification, nitrogen and phosphorus inputs to the biosphere and oceans, aerosol loading and chemical pollution. According to the authors of the paper, three of these planetary boundaries have already been transgressed: climate change, biological diversity and nitrogen input to the biosphere. Since the boundaries are strongly connected, crossing one boundary may seriously threaten our ability to stay within safe levels of the others. The extent to which human societies will be affected by transgressing these planetary boundaries will be dependent on their ability to cope with rapid environmental change. It is often the poorest communities, with weak infrastructures and social support services, which are most at risk.

This scientific evidence points to an age of ecological overshoot, increasing global temperatures, biodiversity loss and environmental pollution. In the face of these challenges, a strong and effective environmental movement is needed. Yet rising environmental scepticism and inconsistent public support for environmental policy measures is further challenging the environmental cause.

Environmental scepticism

Since the 1970s, the US conservative movement has been increasing its opposition to environmentalism. In the 1990s, environmentalism began to develop as a strong global phenomenon epitomised by the 1992 Rio Earth Summit. Some saw this as a threat to the spread of global capitalism and free trade. This, together with the end of the Cold War and the breakdown of the Soviet Union, saw the conservative movement replacing the 'red' scare with a 'green' scare. Conservative opposition began to manifest itself in the form of conservative think tanks sponsored by corporate organisations and foundations. Conservative think tanks have coordinated an anti-environmental counter-movement which has successfully promoted environmental scepticism.[6] Environmental scepticism is strongest in the USA, but is now increasing in other parts of the world, especially with regard to climate change (see Chapter 4). Environmental sceptics tend to deny the seriousness of environmental problems, dismiss scientific evidence, and question the importance of environmental protection policies. Bjørn Lomborg, for example, challenges the priority given by public policy to environmental problems. He argues that environmental concerns are based on myths, and warns: 'when we are told that something is a problem we need to ask how important it is in relation to other problems'.[7] The anti-environmental movement has contributed to the decline in public support for environmental protection policies, and is one reason why the USA failed to ratify the Kyoto Protocol to reduce greenhouse gas emissions.[8] In order to counter such views, environmentalists may need to clarify their worldview and undertake, among other things, an internal debate about the role of technology in addressing new global environmental challenges

The role of technology

Environmentalists have traditionally been suspicious of new technology and have rejected calls to embrace technologies such as GM crops and nuclear power. Many environmentalists have been opposed to nuclear power due to the problems associated with the disposal of nuclear waste and fears of nuclear weapon proliferation and terrorist attack. Some within the movement now believe this is an outdated ideological opposition to technology-based solutions. James Lovelock, creator of the Gaia hypothesis, believes 'opposition to nuclear energy is based on irrational fear fed by Hollywood-style fiction, the Green lobbies and the media. These fears are unjustified, and nuclear energy from its start in 1952 has proved to be the safest of all energy sources.'[9]

American environmentalist Stewart Brand (b. 1938) argues that many of his peers have failed to embrace technologies, and as a consequence this has hindered environmental and social progress, especially in the developing world. In his book *Whole Earth Discipline: An Ecopragmatist Manifesto* (2009) Brand argues that humanity will be saved from climate change by densely populated cities, nuclear energy, GM food and planet-wide geo-engineering to manipulate the Earth's climate to counteract global warming. He has been criticised for assuming technology will solve all political and economic problems while ignoring the issue of power – especially in the context of developing countries.[10]

Environmentalism has always seen splits between those who are technological optimists and those who are wary of what they call 'faulty technology'. The challenge for environmentalists is to come to some level of agreement regarding how their worldview can be made synonymous with progress. Technology undeniably has a role to play in solving many of the world's environmental problems. The environmental movement needs to decide which technologies it is going to support so that it has a positive story to tell. This is a challenge that was taken up by organisations such as Worldchanging, a media organisation that sought to promote 'ideas for building a better future' (2003–10).

Winning hearts and minds

Despite many achievements, contemporary environmentalism has failed to win hearts and minds of a large part of the electorate. Some critics argue the environmental movement is too single-issue focused. The prominence of climate change and the emphasis on reducing emissions has been to the detriment of other environmental issues. While green culture has become mainstream, the extent to which green attitudes have been translated into real action is under question. There has been a tendency for environmentalists to scare people into change. This has been demonstrated by the often alarmist campaigning on climate change. A 2006 study on how the UK media, government and environmental groups communicated climate change found the discussion of climate change issues was 'confusing, contradictory and chaotic, and with the likely result that the public feels disempowered and uncompelled to act'.[11] There is now growing recognition of the need to reframe environmental campaigns that attempt to foster pro-environmental behavioural change. This means providing a positive agenda for the future that focuses on human wellbeing. There are calls for the environmental movement to engage people on the level of values and beliefs and the desire for people to change their own behaviour, to achieve a better quality of life, or to demand change from politicians and business leaders.[12]

Tom Crompton and Tim Kasser (b. 1966) examined the challenges for environmental campaigning in *Meeting Environmental Challenges: The Role of Human Identity* (2009). They argue that the environmental movement has failed to consider human identity in its efforts to change the policies and practices of government and business, as well as the behaviours of individuals. Crompton and Kasser see human identity as a person's sense of him or herself. They highlight three aspects of human identity associated with decisions that often serve to frustrate optimal responses to environmental challenges. These are: people's values and life goals; their differentiation of others into in-groups and out-groups; and the ways they cope with fear and threats. They outline a number of strategies they claim are far more effective than current campaigning approaches. They conclude: 'we believe that the environmental movement cannot fully contribute to creating the systemic changes needed in response to today's environmental challenges unless it understands the problems posed by values and identity, and unless it promotes environmentally beneficial aspects of identity at a societal level.'[13]

Post-environmentalism

Over the past fifty years, the political landscape has changed radically and environmental issues have become more complex and global in nature, requiring a greater transformation of society. Economic growth, consumerism and corporate power are key challenges for the environmental movement. While mainstream politics and business organisation have embraced the need to tackle climate change and achieve a low-carbon and sustainable society, they continue to operate within and promote the existing growth paradigm. Focusing on specific actions such as reducing emissions without challenging this paradigm is seen by some environmentalists as futile. They argue that the environmental movement has been naive to think that 'sound science' and appealing to a collective self-interest is sufficient to push for change against ideological and industrial opposition. Instead, they call for environmentalism to be rooted in fundamental value change and a systematic transformation of economy, politics and culture – essentially an ecological revolution.

To achieve a transition to a new ecological age on the scale of the industrial revolution requires a strong and effective environmental movement that can set out a vision of a desirable and compelling future. Ted Nordhaus and Michael Shellenberger (b. 1971) have criticised the environmental movement for failing to be a vital force for cultural and social change, in their controversial essay entitled *The Death of Environmentalism* (2004), quoted at the start of this chapter, and in their 2007 book *Break Through: From the Death of Environmentalism to the Politics of Possibility*.[14] They argue for a positive 'post-environmental' politics where environmentalism must abandon its focus on nature and be reborn as a new progressive politics that focuses on sustainable economy. Nordhaus and Shellenberger suggest that environmentalists limit and constrain human power rather than unleashing human ingenuity and endeavour. They argue:

> It is our contention that we have to begin building the new energy economy before we can tear down the old one. We believe that the same thing is true of the new politics. We need to create a politics of possibility to replace the old politics of limits.[15]

A 'politics of possibility' requires abandoning traditional opposition between business and the environment, humans and nature, government and markets, and replacing it with 'more expansive, pragmatic and holistic solutions'. Following this argument, climate change should not be seen as a pollution problem similar to acid rain, smog and depletion of the ozone layer, each of which required relatively simple and inexpensive technical fixes such as catalytic converters and scrubbers on power plants. Instead, climate change requires a new kind of economic development and technological innovation – one that focuses on major public investments to make cheaper solar, wind, hydrogen and bio-fuels and cleaner coal.

Nordhaus and Shellenberger contend that: 'modern environmentalism, with all of its unexamined assumptions, outdated concepts and exhausted strategies, must die so that something new can live'.[16] These arguments have been seen as 'highly problematic' and questionable in several areas. For example, they suggest reforming the capitalist system without significant changes in lifestyles or consumption patterns. Research also shows that fear of environmental destruction can be effective in inducing individuals to join and support environmental organisations if it is combined with information on what can be done about it. A combination of threats and opportunities – 'nightmares' combined with 'dreams' – can mobilise people to take action.[17]

A new age of environmental localism

As the world enters an age of natural resource scarcity and climate change, food and energy insecurity will affect the way of life of local communities. The unpredictable effects of climate change will further exacerbate these scarcity challenges. At the height of the 2007 food price hike, *Financial Times* journalist Martin Wolf observed:

> the biggest point about debates on climate change and energy supply is that they bring back the question of limits. This is why climate change and energy security are such geopolitically significant issues. For if there are limits to emissions, there may also be limits to growth. But if there are indeed limits to growth, the political underpinnings of our world fall apart. Intense distributional conflicts must then re-emerge – indeed, they are already emerging – within and among countries.[18]

The root of many environmental problems lies in the inherent social injustices that are perpetuated from one generation to the next. Development has often been seen as a way to eradicating poverty.[19] However, while this has improved living standards for the few, it has often created inequities within society. Evidence suggests that more equal societies always do better both socially and environmentally.[20] In an age of fiscal austerity, resource scarcity and climate change, redefining prosperity and moving away from conspicuous consumption to local collaborative consumption (for example, with regard to energy, transport and food) could be the key to addressing environmental challenges.

This will require a greater focus on grassroots action and 'green localism' that could re-engage a public that is sometimes disinterested in and suspicious of environmental issues. The notion of 'decentralisation' is not a new concept, and has been at the heart of the environmental movement, reflecting its commitment to localism balanced by global responsibility. Empowering community groups and strengthening community bonds could deliver multiple social and environmental benefits. People could be encouraged to take action to tackle issues that are local priorities and within their immediate sphere of influence. By working in partnership with local authorities and businesses, local groups could contribute to building community resilience by becoming more self-sufficient. This would enable local communities to tackle climate change, improve health and wellbeing, secure a healthy natural environment and become safer and more cohesive. There are already many groups and projects that are 'acting locally and thinking globally', such as cooperatives, transition towns and neighbourhood schemes.

A new form of environmentalism is required for a new age of global challenges, one that addresses the impact that global food and energy insecurity and climate change will have on local communities. The environmental movement has the potential to evolve through a network of grassroots groups that contribute to national and international campaigns using social media and internet technology.

Whether the environmental movement can continue to be a force for change in the twenty-first century is dependent on whether evolution will come naturally to what is still a relatively young social movement. Is environmentalism now too institutionalised and wedded to the successes of the 1960s to change? It remains to be seen how the environmental idea can be captured and shaped by new generations in an age of new environmental challenges. What seems certain is that the whole of society will have to develop ways to respond to the profound effects that future global environmental change will have on our current way of life.

Notes

1 Introduction

1 R. Bendiner, 'Man – The Most Endangered Species', *New York Times*, 20 October 1969.
2 E. Goldsmith, R. Allen, M. Allaby, J. Davoll and S. Lawrence (eds), 'A Blueprint for Survival', *The Ecologist*, 2(1), 1972, www.theecologist.org/back_archive/19701999/.
3 John Hannigan and many other writers describe these strands of thought as discourses, each with their own history, writers, imagery and events. The strands listed here are similar to those that R. J. Brulle associates with the history of American environmentalism. See J. Hannigan, *Environmental Sociology*, 2nd edn, London: Routledge, 2006, pp. 36–52.
4 See for example D. Pepper, *The Roots of Modern Environmentalism*, Kent: Croom Helm, 1984.
5 Quoted in J. Radku, translated by T. Dunlap, *Nature and Power: A Global History of the Environment*, Cambridge: Cambridge University Press, 1998.
6 Donald Worster describes the 'age of ecology' as beginning with the detonation of the first atomic bomb in a desert in New Mexico on 16 July 1945. See D. Worster, *Nature's Economy: A History of Ecological Ideas*, Cambridge: Cambridge University Press, 1998, p. 342.

2 The environmental movement

1 A number of studies point towards the growth of the environmental movement globally. The World Values Survey shows increases in self-reported membership of environmental organisations for some countries since 1981. See R. J. Dalton, 'The Greening of the Globe? Cross-national Levels of Environmental Group Membership', *Environmental Politics*, 14(4), 2005, pp. 441–59.
2 L. Martell, *Ecology and Society: An Introduction*, London: Polity Press, 1994.
3 These social movements mainly supported issues such as workers' rights, gender equality and electoral representation. See C. Tilly, *Social Movements, 1768–2004*, London: Paradigm, 2004, pp. 48–64.
4 These are the words of Wordsworth, who was writing about the Lake District in northern England. His sentiment was echoed by nineteenth-century writers in the USA, including Ralph Waldo Emerson, Henry David Thoreau

and John Muir. See W. A. Wordsworth, *Guide Through the District of the Lakes in the North of England, With a Description of the Scenery*, Kendal: Hudson and Nicholson, 1835.
5 M. Castells, *The Power of Identity*, Oxford: Blackwell, 2004, pp. 168–79.
6 H. Ritvo, *Dawn of Green: Manchester, Thirlmere and Modern Environmentalism*, Chicago: Chicago University Press, 2009, p. 171.
7 R. W. Righter, *The Battle over Hetch Hetchy: America's Most Controversial Dam and the Birth of Modern Environmentalism*, Oxford: Oxford University Press, 2005, pp. 25, 73.
8 C. Rootes, *Nature Protection Organizations in England*, Working Paper 1, Centre for the Study of Social and Political Movements, School of Social Policy, Sociology and Social Research, University of Kent at Canterbury, 2007, www.kent.ac.uk/sspssr/research/papers/rootes-nat-pro-england.pdf.
9 For Sierra Club membership figures, together with those of other American groups from 1950 onwards, see B. Straughan and T. Pollak, *The Broader Movement: Nonprofit Environmental and Conservation Organizations, 1989–2005*, Washington, DC: National Centre for Charitable Statistics at the Urban Institute, 2005, p. 49, www.urban.org/publications/411797.html.
10 For RSPB membership figure, see RSPB website, 'Timeline and milestones', www.rspb.org.uk/about/history/milestones.aspx.
11 The organisation's international secretariat was established in Switzerland in September 1961, and national WWF offices were gradually set up across the world, starting with the UK in November 1961.
12 This was a syndicated Associated Press article, but the *Daily News* ran with the title 'Revolt of the Bird Watchers'. See S. Benjamin, 'Revolt of the Birdwatchers: Environmental Lawsuits on Increase', *Daily News*, 27 December 1971, p. 35.
13 E. Russell, *War and Nature, Fighting Humans and Insects with Chemicals from World War I to Silent Spring*, Cambridge: Cambridge University Press, 2001, pp. 166–221.
14 Friends of the Earth, '21 years of Friends of the Earth', London: Friends of the Earth, 1992.
15 J. Bulger, 'Friends of the Earth is 10 years old', *New Scientist*, 30 April 1989, p. 296.
16 M. Bennulf, 'The rise and fall of *Miljöpartiet de gröna*' in D. Richardson and C. Rootes (eds), *The Green Challenge: The Development of Green Parties in Europe*, London: Routledge, 1995, pp. 128–46.
17 *Miljöpartiet de gröna* website, www.mp.se/templates/Mct_177.aspx?number=184753.
18 E. Gene Frankland, 'Germany: The Rise, Fall and Recovery of Die Grunen' in D. Richardson and C. Rootes (eds), *The Green Challenge: The Development of Green Parties in Europe*, London: Routledge, 1995, pp. 23–45.
19 J. McCormick, *The Global Environmental Movement*, London: Belhaven Press, 1989, pp. 137–43.
20 By this time the Ecology Party had become the Green Party.
21 World Wide Fund for Nature website, http://wwf.panda.org/who_we_are/history/sixties/.
22 C. Hails, 'WWF from 1961 to 2006: WWF's approach to conservation from its inception to 2006', http://wwf.panda.org/who_we_are/history/wwf_conservation_1961_2006/.

23 Ben Metcalfe, quoted in R. Weyler, *Greenpeace: How a Group of Journalists, Ecologists and Visionaries Changed the World*, Vancouver: Raincoast Books, 2004, p. 95.
24 P. Wapner, 'Politics Beyond the State: Environmental Activism and World Civic Politics', *World Politics*, 47(3), 1995, pp. 311–40.
25 L. W. Cole and S. R. Foster, *From the Ground Up: Environmental Racism and the Rise of the Environmental Justice Movement*, New York: New York University Press, 2001.
26 G. McKay, *Senseless Acts of Beauty: Cultures of Resistance since the Sixties*, London: Verso, 1996.
27 Commission for Racial Justice, *Toxic Wastes and Race in the United States: A National Report on the Racial and Socio-Economic Characteristics of Communities with Hazardous Waste Sites*, New York: Commission for Racial Justice, United Church of Christ, 1987, www.ucc.org/about-us/archives/pdfs/toxwrace87.pdf.
28 R. D. Bullard, *Confronting Environmental Racism: Voices from the Grassroots*, Cambridge: South End Press, 1993.
29 Department of the Environment, *This Common Inheritance: Britain's Environmental Strategy*, London: HMSO, 1990.
30 G. Rice, 'Opening up the Bank', in R. Cagia (ed.), *Balancing the Development Agenda: The Transformation of the World Bank under James D Wolfensohn*, Washington, DC: World Bank, 2005, p. 76.
31 The G8 are Canada, France, Germany, Italy, Japan, Russia, USA and UK.
32 Indymedia UK, 'Reporting Large Scale Events', www.indymedia.org.uk/en/static/about_us.html.
33 The events were widely reported at the time and the police were subjected to a number of investigations. See for example N. Davies, 'The Bloody Battle of Genoa', *The Guardian*, 17 July 2008, www.guardian.co.uk/world/2008/jul/17/italy.g8.
34 For the basis of the American estimate see Straughan and Pollak, *The Broader Movement: Nonprofit Environmental and Conservation Organizations, 1989–2005, op. cit.*, p. 49. The UK estimate is based on a 2007 press release from the Green Alliance on behalf of a number of environmental organisations in the UK, 'UK Political Parties Fall Short of The Green Standard', www.green-alliance.org.uk/grea1.aspx?id=2174.
35 Each of these examples is a story in itself; the references that follow (notes 35–42) provide a sample of the different ways Greenpeace and multinational corporations have interacted and the different ways the outcomes have been reported.
36 G. Tyler, 'Bayer Finally Gets the Message: We Don't Want GE!' Greenpeace, 24 June 2010, www.greenpeace.org/international/en/news/Blogs/makingwaves/bayer-finally-gets-the-message-we-dont-want-g/blog/12546.
37 A. Pasternack, 'Coke's New Vending Machines: Like Taking 218,000 Cars Off The Roads For Two Weeks', Treehugger, 9 April 2008, www.treehugger.com/files/2008/09/coca-cola-green-coolers-vending-machines-hfc-free.php.
38 A. Petrou, 'Dell Faces Greenpeace Wrath', TechEye.net, 26 May 2010, www.techeye.net/business/dell-nintendo-face-greenpeace-wrath.
39 M. Kaufman, 'New Allies on the Amazon: McDonalds, Greenpeace, Unite to Prevent Forest Clearing', *Washington Post*, 24 April 2007, www.washingtonpost.com/wp-dyn/content/article/2007/04/23/AR2007042301903.html.

40 S. Milloy, 'Monsanto Caves to Activists on Biotech Wheat', *Fox News*, 14 May 2004, www.foxnews.com/story/0,2933,119884,00.html.
41 J. Van Grove, 'Nestle meets Greenpeace's demands following social media backlash', Mashable, 17 May 2010, www.mashable.com/2010/05/17/nestle-social-media-fallout.
42 Greenpeace, 'Green My Apple, to the Core', www.greenpeace.org/apple.
43 Greenpeace, 'Green My Apple Bears Fruit', 31 May 2007, www.greenpeace.org/international/greeningofapple.
44 Conservation International History, www.conservation.org/discover/pages/history.aspx.
45 WWF and HSBC, 'Investing in Nature', www.wwf.org.uk/what_we_do/working_with_business/companies_we_work_with/hsbc.cfm.
46 See for example J. Hari, 'The Wrong Kind of Green', *The Nation*, 22 March 2010, www.thenation.com/article/wrong-kind-green.
47 Friends of the Earth, 'Media Briefing: HSBC Financing Forest Destruction and Social Conflict', 28 May 2004, www.foe.co.uk/resource/media_briefing/hsbc_banking_on_palm_oil.pdf.
48 Greenpeace, *Carbon Scam: Noel Kempff Climate Action Project and the Push for Sub-national Forest Offsets*, Amsterdam: Greenpeace International, 2009, www.greenpeace.org/raw/content/usa/press-center/reports4/carbon-scam-noel-kempff-clima.pdf.
49 J. Hoeskstra, 'The Noel Kempff Climate Action Project: The Conservancy Responds to a Greenpeace Report', Cool Green Science, October 2009, blog.nature.org/2009/10/noel-kempff-climate-forest-greenpeace-nature-conservancy.
50 Friends of the Earth, 'Brief history of The Big Ask, Friends of the Earth's climate campaign', July 2007, www.foe.co.uk/resource/media_briefing/brief_history_the_big_ask.pdf.
51 J. Tollefson, 'U.S. Climate Bill Arrives in Senate', *Scientific American*, 12 May 2010, www.scientificamerican.com/article.cfm?id=us-climate-bill-arrives-in-senate.
52 E. Clifton, 'Hopes Fade For Languishing U.S. Climate Bill', Global Issues, 26 July 2010, www.globalissues.org/news/2010/07/26/6418.
53 A list of official Transition Town initiatives can be found at Transition Network, www.transitionnetwork.org/initiatives/by-number?page=10.
54 A. Downs, 'Up and Down with Ecology – the Issue–Attention Cycle', *Public Interest*, 28, 1972, pp. 38–50.

3 Global environmental governance

1 UNESCO, *The Scientific Conference on Resource Conservation and Utilisation (UNSCCUR)*, Paris: United Nations Education and Scientific Organisation, 1948, unesdoc.unesco.org/images/0015/001547/154751eb.pdf.
2 N. Pelletier, 'Of Laws and Limits: An Ecological Economic Perspective on Redressing the Failure of Contemporary Global Environmental Governance', *Global Environmental Change*, 20, 2010, pp. 220–28.
3 F. Carpenter, 'Conservation of World Resources: A Report on UN Scientific Conference', *Bulletin of the Atomic Scientists*, November 1949, 313–14.
4 N. Schrijver, *Sovereignty Over Natural Resources: Balancing Rights and Duties*, Cambridge: Cambridge University Press, 1997.

5 N. Schrijver, J. Crawford and S. Panitchpakdi, *Development without Destruction: The UN and Global Resource Management*, Bloomington: Indiana University Press, 2010, p. 43.
6 United Nations, *Problems of the Human Environment: Report of the Secretary-General*, Forty-seventh Session of the Economic and Social Council, E/4667, 1969.
7 Quoted in M. Ivanova, 'Moving Forward by Looking Back: Learning from UNEP's History', in L. Swart and E. Perry (eds), *Global Environmental Governance: Perspectives on the Current Debate*, New York: Center for UN Reform Education, 2007, pp. 26–47.
8 M. Ivanova, 'UNEP in Global Environmental Governance: Design, Leadership and Location', *Global Environmental Politics*, 10(1), 2010, 30–59.
9 M. Ivanova and J. Roy, 'The Architecture of Global Environmental Governance: Pros and Cons of Multiplicity' in L. Swart and E. Perry (eds) *Global Environmental Governance: Perspectives on the Current Debate*, New York: Center for UN Reform Education, 2007, www.centerforunreform.org/node/251.
10 L. Elliott, *The Global Politics of the Environment*, New York: New York University Press, 1998.
11 A. Najam, 'Developing Countries and Global Environmental Governance: From Contestation to Participation to Engagement', *International Environmental Agreements*, 5, 2005, pp. 303–21.
12 M. Williams, 'Re-articulating the Third World Coalition: The Role of the Environmental Agenda', *Third World Quarterly*, 14(1), 1993, pp. 7–29.
13 M. K. Tolba, O. A. El-Kholy, E. El-Hinnawi, M. W. Holgate, D. F. McMichael and R. E. Munn, *The World Environment 1972–1992: Two Decades of Challenge*, London: Chapman & Hall, 1992.
14 M. G. Schecter, *United Nations Global Conferences*, London: Routledge, 2005.
15 UNEP, *Environmental Law Training Manual*, Nairobi: United Nations Environment Programme, 1992.
16 Ivanova, 2007, op. cit.
17 Centre for Global Negotiations, 'The Brandt Equation: 21st Century Blueprint for the New Global Economy', www.brandt21forum.info/About_BrandtCommission.htm).
18 J. B. Quilligan, 'The Superbubble behind "The Great Moderation:" How the Brandt Report Foresaw Today's Global Economic Crisis', *Integral Review*, 6(1), 2010, www.integral-review.org/documents/Quilligan,%20The%20Superbubble%20behind%20The%20Great%20Moderation,%20Vol.%206%20No.%201.pdf.
19 W. Brandt, *The Brandt Commission. Common Crisis: North–South Cooperation for World Recovery*, Boston: MIT Press, 1983.
20 UN Documents website, 'Resolutions adopted by the General Assembly 38/161. Process of preparation of the Environmental Perspective to the Year 2000 and Beyond', www.un-documents.net/a38r161.
21 The International Union for Conservation of Nature and Natural Resources (IUCN) in collaboration with UNESCO, UNEP and WWF.
22 IUCN, *The World Conservation Strategy*, Gland: International Union for the Conservation of Nature, 1980.
23 World Commission on Environment and Development, *Our Common Future*, Oxford: Oxford University Press, 1987.

24 J. Elkington, 'Brundtland and sustainability: history's balance-sheet', Open Democracy, 11 April 2007, www.opendemocracy.net/globalization-institutions_government/sustainability_4521.jsp.
25 S. Daley, 'Reading Rio, Writing the World: *The New York Times* and the "Earth Summit"', *Political Geography*, 15(6/7), 1996, pp. 593–613.
26 Earth Summit, www.un.org/geninfo/bp/enviro.html.
27 J. Madeley, 'Earth Summit Overlooks Poverty Now', *Land Use Policy*, October 1992, pp. 300–302.
28 *Ibid*.
29 Maurice Strong.net, 'The Earth Summit: Introduction', www.mauricestrong.net/20100716167/rio/rio/introduction.html.
30 K. Conca, 'Environmental Governance after Johannesburg: From Stalled Legalization to Environmental Human Rights?', *Journal of International Law & International Relations*, 1(1/2), 2005, pp. 121–38.
31 D. G. Victor, 'Recovering Sustainable Development', *Foreign Affairs*, 85(1), 2006, pp. 91–103.
32 R. Mikkelsen, 'Bush to Skip Earth Summit', *Global Policy Forum*, 12 August 2002, www.globalpolicy.org/component/content/article/212/45436.html.
33 J. Swatuk, 'From Rio to Johannesburg and Beyond: Way Forward for the post-WSSD Commonwealth', *The Roundtable*, 371, 2003, pp. 465–75.
34 B. H. Desai, *Multilateral Environmental Agreements: Legal Status of the Secretariats*, Cambridge: Cambridge University Press, 2010, p. 48.
35 T. Sandler, *Global Collective Action*, Cambridge: Cambridge University Press, 2004.
36 IPCC, *Climate Change 1995. The Science of Climate Change, Contribution of Working Group I to the Second Assessment Report of the Intergovernmental Panel on Climate Change*, Cambridge: Cambridge University Press, 1995.
37 IPCC, *Climate Change 2007: The Physical Science Basis. Contribution of Working Group I to the Fourth Assessment Report of the Intergovernmental Panel on Climate Change*, Cambridge: Cambridge University Press, 2007.
38 The Nobel Peace Prize, '2007 – Prize Announcement', www.nobelprize.org/nobel_prizes/peace/laureates/2007/announcement.html.
39 Ivanova, 'Moving Forward by Looking Back: Learning from UNEP's History', op. cit.
40 R. N. Haas, 'The Age of Nonpolarity: What Will Follow US Dominance?', *Foreign Affairs*, May/June 2008.
41 Pricewaterhousecoopers, 'Cancun: G20 Growth Race Is On', www.ukmediacentre.pwc.com/content/Detail.aspx?ReleaseID=4011&NewsAreaID=2.

4 Science and the environment

1 P. Findlen, 'Natural History', in K. Park and L. Dalston (eds), *The Cambridge History of Science Volume 3: Early Modern Science*, Cambridge: Cambridge University Press, 2006, pp. 435–38.
2 F. N. Egerton, *History of American Ecology*, North Stratford, NH: Ayer Company, 1984, pp. 311–36.
3 This was set out towards the end of Thoreau's life, in books such as *The Succession of Forest Trees*, published in 1860.
4 C. Merchant, *Radical Ecology: The Search for a Liveable World*, London: Routledge, 1992, p. 75.

5 N. W. Moore, *The Bird of Time: The Science and Politics of Nature Conservation*, Cambridge: Cambridge University Press, 1987, pp. 150–54.
6 R. Carson, *Silent Spring*, London: Penguin Classics, 2000, pp. 56–60.
7 E. Russell, *War and Nature: Fighting Humans and Insects with Chemicals from World War I to Silent Spring*, Cambridge: Cambridge University Press, 2001, p. 221.
8 This is taken from the history of Greenpeace by R. Weyler, *Greenpeace: How a Group of Journalists, Ecologists and Visionaries Changed the World*, Vancouver, Raincoast Books, 2004.
9 B. Tokar, *Earth for Sale: Reclaiming Ecology in the Age of Corporate Greenwash*, Cambridge, MA: South End Press, 1997, p. 115.
10 Bookchin actually preferred the term 'ecologism' to 'environmentalism', though the distinction he makes between the two terms is not widely recognised outside academia.
11 J. Lovelock, 'The Independent Practice of Science', *New Scientist*, 6 September 1979, pp. 714–17.
12 John Hannigan describes how environmental proposals need to be compatible with the values of policy makers in J. Hannigan, *Environmental Sociology*, London: Routledge, 2006, pp. 73–74.
13 E. O. Wilson discusses the number of recognised living species in the world in E. O. Wilson, *The Diversity of Life*, new edn, London: Penguin, 2001, pp. xi–xii.
14 The Red Books have been replaced by the IUCN Red List, which classifies species into eight categories of risk, designed to help policy makers plan and prioritise conservation efforts and to communicate biodiversity loss to the public. Another way of prioritising biodiversity conservation on a global scale was introduced by the British ecologist Norman Myers. He defined the biodiversity hotspot concept in 1988 to describe areas with exceptionally high levels of endemic species that are under threat, so shifting the policy focus from species to ecosystems.
15 Known as the SCOPE 29 report: B. Bolin, B. J. Jager and J. Doos, *Scope 29: The Greenhouse Effect, Climate Change, and Ecosystems*, Chichester: John Wiley & Sons, 1986.
16 The number of science journals rose from fewer than 100 in 1990 to over 500 in the year 2000. From Goodall, referenced in M. Hulme, *Why We Disagree about Climate Change: Understanding Controversy, Inaction and Opportunity*, Cambridge: Cambridge University Press, 2009, p. 66.
17 UNEP, *Global Environmental Outlook 3: Executive Summary*, www.cbd.int/gbo/gbo3/doc/GBO3-Summary-final-en.pdf.
18 F. Pearce, *Acid Rain: What Is It, And What Is It Doing To Us?* London: Penguin, 1987, p. 29.
19 *Ibid.*, p. 133
20 These examples are taken from a wide-ranging CBC radio interview with the Canadian scientist Harold Harvey, conducted on 30 June 1991. See CBC, 'Acid Rain: Pollution and Politics', http://archives.cbc.ca/environment/pollution/topics/584/.
21 Quoted in C. Park, *Acid Rain: Rhetoric and Reality*, London: Methuen, 1987, p. 180.
22 S. Jasanoff, *Designs on Nature: Science and Democracy in Europe and the United States*, Princeton, NJ: Princeton University Press, 2005.

23 N. Nuttall, 'Silent Spring 2020', *The Times*, 13 July 1998, p. 15.
24 D. Toke, *The Politics of GM Food: A Comparative Study of the UK, USA and EU*, London: Routledge, 2004.
25 S. Yearley, *Cultures of Environmentalism: Empirical Studies in Environmental Sociology*, Basingstoke: Palgrave Macmillan, 2005, pp. 144–58.
26 S. Schneider, 'No Deception in Global Warming Report', Letter to the Editor of *The Wall Street Journal*, 1996, http://stephenschneider.stanford.edu/Publications/PDF_Papers/WSJ_June25.pdf.
27 *Ibid.*
28 Hulme, *Why We Disagree about Climate Change: Understanding Controversy, Inaction and Opportunity*, op. cit., pp. 93–95.
29 M. Russell, G. Boulton, P. Clarke, D. Eyton and J. Norton, *The Independent Climate Change E-mails Review*, July 2010, p. 11, www.cce-review.org.
30 G. Monbiot, 'With Complex Science, We Must Take Much On Trust. The Trouble Is We Can't', *The Guardian*, 9 March 2010, p. 27.
31 Wilson, *The Diversity of Life*, op cit., p. 24.

5 Economics and the environment

1 F. Ackerman, *Can We Afford the Future? The Economics of a Warming World*, London: Zed Books, 2009, p. 12.
2 A. Smith, *An Inquiry into the Nature and Causes of the Wealth of Nations: A Selected Edition*, K. Sutherland (ed.), Oxford: Oxford University Press, 1776/1993, p. 50.
3 Smith and Sutherland, *An Inquiry into the Nature and Causes of the Wealth of Nations*, op. cit., p. 448.
4 D. Harvey, *The Limits to Capital*, London: Verso, 2006, pp. 334–35.
5 E. Kula, *Economics of Natural Resources, the Environment and Policies*, London: Chapman & Hall, 1997.
6 J. S. Mill, *Principles of Political Economy with some of their Applications to Social Philosophy*, London: Penguin, 1970, p. 111.
7 D. W. Pearce and R. K. Turner, *Economics of Natural Resources and the Environment*, Hemel Hempstead: Harvester Wheatsheaf, 1990.
8 J. K. Galbraith, *The Affluent Society*, London: Penguin, 1999, p. 101.
9 R. L. Bradley, *Capitalism at Work: Business, Government, and Energy*, Salem, MA: Scrivener Press, 2009.
10 Quoted in P. Desrochers and C. Hoffbauer, 'The Post War Intellectual Roots of the Population Bomb', *Electronic Journal of Sustainable Development*, 1(3), 2009, 37–61, www.ejsd.org/public/journal_article/12.
11 P. R. Ehrlich and A. H. Ehrlich, 'The Population Bomb Revisited', *Electronic Journal of Sustainable Development*, 1(3), 2009, 63–71, www.ejsd.org/docs/The_Population_Bomb_Revisited.pdf.
12 T. O'Riordan and K. Turner, *An Annotated Reader in Environmental Planning and Management*, Oxford: Pergamon, 1983.
13 R. S. Deese, 'The Artifact of Nature: "Spaceship Earth" and the dawn of global environmentalism', *Endeavour*, 33(2), 2009, pp. 70–75.
14 P. R. Ehrlich and J. P. Holdren, 'A Bulletin Dialogue Critique: One Dimensional Ecology', *Bulletin of the Atomic Scientists*, May 1972, pp. 16–27.
15 J. F. Kennedy Presidential Library and Museum, 'Remarks of Robert F. Kennedy at the University of Kansas, March 18, 1968', www.jfklibrary.org/

Historical+Resources/Archives/Reference+Desk/Speeches/RFK/RFKSpeech68Mar18UKansas.htm.
16. R. Costanza, R. Leemans, R. Boumans and E. Gaddis, 'Integrated Global Models', in W. Steffen (ed.), *Sustainability or Collapse? An Integrated History and Future of People on Earth*, Cambridge, MA: MIT Press, 2007, pp. 417–46.
17. See Club of Rome, 'The Story of the Club of Rome', www.clubofrome.org/eng/about/4.
18. D. H. Meadows, D. L. Meadows, J. Randers and W. W. Behrens III, *The Limits to Growth*, New York: Universe Books, 1972.
19. See for example P. Lawn, 'On the Ehrlich–Simon Bet: Both were Unskilled and Simon was Lucky', *Ecological Economics*, 69(11), 2010, pp. 2045–46.
20. H. E. Daly and J. B. Cobb Jr, *For the Common Good: Redirecting the Economy Towards Community, the Environment and a Sustainable Future*, London: Green Print, 1990, pp. 194–97.
21. J. Gowdy and S. Mesner, 'The Evolution of Georgescu-Roegen's Bioeconomics', *Review of Social Economy*, 56(2), 1998, pp. 136–56.
22. H. E. Daly, *A Steady-State Economy*, London: Sustainable Development Commission, 2008, www.sd-commission.org.uk/publications.php?id=775.
23. M. Waring, *Counting for Nothing: What Men Value and What Women are Worth*, Toronto: Toronto University Press, 1999.
24. H. E. Daly and J. B. Cobb Jr, *For the Common Good: Redirecting the Economy Towards Community, the Environment and a Sustainable Future*, London: Green Print, 1990, pp. 401–55.
25. World Bank, 'Global Partnership for Wealth Accounting and the Valuation of Ecosystem Services (WAVES)', go.worldbank.org/PL08P9FTN0.
26. See C. C. Park, *Acid Rain: Rhetoric and Reality*, London: Methuen, 1987, pp. 122–23.
27. N. Georgescu-Roegen, *Energy and Economic Myths*, New York: Pergamon, 1976, p. xix.
28. H. Mooney and P. R. Ehrlich, 'Ecosystem Services: A Fragmentary History', in G. C. Daily, *Nature's Services: Societal Dependence on Natural Ecosystems*, Washington, DC: Island Press, 1997, pp. 14–15.
29. Millennium Ecosystem Assessment, *Ecosystems and Human Well-being: Synthesis*, Washington, DC: Island Press, 2005.
30. R. Costanza, R. d'Arge, R. de Groot, S. Parber, M. Grasso, B. Hannon, K. Limburg, S. Naeem, R. V. O'Neil, J. Paruelo, R. G. Raskin, P. Sutton and M. van den Belt, 'The Value of the World's Ecosystem Services and Natural Capital', *Nature*, 387, 1987, 253–60, www.ecy.wa.gov.programs/wr/hq/pdf/naturepaper.pdf.
31. N. Stern, *The Economics of Climate Change: The Stern Review*, Cambridge: Cambridge University Press, 2006, p. 27.
32. Ackerman *Can We Afford the Future? The Economics of a Warming World*, op. cit., pp. 15–27.
33. W. Nordhaus, *A Question of Balance: Weighing the Options of Global Warming Policies*, London: Yale University Press, 2008.
34. Ackerman, *Can We Afford the Future? The Economics of a Warming World*, op. cit., p. 18.
35. J. Eliasch, *Climate Change: Financing Global Forests, The Eliasch Review*, London: Earthscan, 2008.

36 UNEP Finance Initiative/PRI, 'Universal Ownership: Why Environmental Externalities Matter to Institutional Investors', www.unepfi.org/fileadmin/documents/universal_ownership.pdf.
37 For more on this, see Pavan Sukhdev, Heidi Wittmer, Christoph Schröter-Schlaack, Carsten Nesshöver, Joshua Bishop, Patrick ten Brink, Haripriya Gundimeda, Pushpam Kumar and Ben Simmons, *Mainstreaming the Economics of Nature: A Synthesis of the Approach, Conclusions and Recommendations of TEEB*, Bonn: The Economics of Systems and Biodiversity, www.teebweb.org/TEEBSynthesisReport/tabid/29410/Default.aspx.
38 G. Hardin, 'The Tragedy of the Commons', *Science*, 162(3859), 1968, pp. 1243–48.
39 I. R. Calder, *The Blue Revolution: Land Use and Integrated Water Resources Management*, London: Earthscan, 1999.
40 P. H. Gleick, G. Wolff, E. L. Chalecki and R. Reyes, 'Globalisation and International Trade of Water', in P. H. Gleick (ed.), *The World's Water: The Biennial Report on Freshwater Resources 2002–2003*, London: Island Press, pp. 33–56.
41 E. Ostrom, J. Burger, C. B. Field, R. B. Norgaard and D. Policansky, 'Revisiting the Commons: Local Lessons, Global Challenge', *Science*, 278 (5412), 1999, pp. 278–82.
42 E. Ostrom, *The Evolution of Institutions for Collective Action*, Cambridge: Cambridge University Press, 1990.
43 World Bank, *Global Economic Prospects 2009. Commodities at the Crossroads*, Washington, DC: The World Bank, 2009.
44 UNEP, *Global Green New Deal*, Nairobi: United Nations Environment Programme, 2009.
45 The G20 accounts for two-thirds of the world population, 90 per cent of global activity and nearly 75 per cent of global greenhouse gas emissions.
46 G20, 'Leaders' Statement – The Global Plan for Recovery and Reform', London, 2 April 2009, www.g20.org/pub_communiques.aspx.
47 G20, 'Leaders' Statement, The Pittsburgh Summit', Pittsburgh, pp. 24–25 September 2009, www.g20.org/pub_communiques.aspx.
48 E. B. Barbier, 'Global Governance: The G20 and a Global Green New Deal', *Economics E-Journal*, 4, 13 January 2010, www.economics-ejournal.org/economics/journalarticles/2010-2.
49 E. B. Barbier, 'Dealing in Green: A global recovery strategy', *The Broker*, 20/21, July 2010.
50 UNEP, *Towards a Green Economy: Pathways To Sustainable Development and Poverty Eradication*, Nairobi: United Nations Environment Programme, 2011.
51 T. Jackson, *Prosperity Without Growth: Economics for a Finite Planet*, London: Earthscan, 2009.
52 NEF, *Growth Isn't Working*, London: New Economics Foundation, 2006.
53 OECD, 'Indicators to Measure Decoupling of Environmental Pressure from Economic Growth', Paris: Organisation for Economic Co-operation and Development, 2002, www.oecd.org/dataoecd/0/52/1933638.pdf.

6 Popular culture and environment

1 E. Kaledin, *Daily Life in the United States, 1940–1959: Shifting Worlds*, Westport, CT: Greenwood Press, 2000, p. 55.

2 D. Starke, *The Motorway Age: Road and Traffic Policies in Post-War Britain*, Oxford: Pergamon, 1982.
3 R. Meyer, 'A History of Green Brands 1960s and 1970s – Doing the Groundwork', Fast Company, www.fastcompany.com/1568686/keen-to-be-green-50-years-of-people-planet-and-profits.
4 V. Lebow, 'Price Competition in 1955', *Journal of Retailing*, Spring, 1955, http://hundredgoals.files.wordpress.com/2009/05/journal-of-retailing.pdf.
5 J. K. Galbraith, *The Affluent Society*, London: Penguin, 1999, pp. 187–88.
6 B. Black, *Nature and the Environment in Twentieth Century American Life*, Westport, CT: Greenwood Press, 2006, p. 143.
7 R. Poole, *Earthrise: How Man First Saw the Earth*, Yale, CT: Yale University Press.
8 *Ibid*.
9 'Richard Nixon's First State of the Union Address', http://en.wikisource.org/wiki/Richard_Nixon%27s_First_State_of_the_Union_Address.
10 R. Earle, *The Art of Cause Marketing: How to Use Advertising to Change Personal Behaviour and Public Policy*, New York: McGraw Hill, 2000, pp. 69–71.
11 Keep America Beautiful, www.kab.org/site/PageServer?pagename=kab_history.
12 Department of Environmental Quality, 'Oregon Bottle Bill, Then and Now', www.deq.state.or.us/lq/sw/bottlebill/thenandnow.htm.
13 Container Recycling Institute, 'Keep America Beautiful: A History', http://toolkit.bottlebill.org/opposition/KABhistory.htm.
14 Institute for Local Self-Reliance, *Beyond 40 Percent. Record-Setting Recycling and Composting Programs*, Washington, DC: Island Press, 1991.
15 Ecology Center, 'Our History', www.ecologycenter.org/about/whoweare.html.
16 British Glass, 'The Bottle Bank Celebrates Its 25th Birthday', August 2002, www.britglass.org.uk/newsevents/BGNewsArchive/TheBottleBankCelebratesIt.html.
17 F. Ackerman, *Why Do We Recycle: Markets, Values and Public Policy?*, Washington, DC: Island Press, 1997, pp. 110–11.
18 Ethical Consumer, 'Successful Consumer Boycotts', www.ethicalconsumer.org/Boycotts/successfulboycotts.aspx.
19 J. Elkington and T. Burke, *The Green Capitalists*, London: Victor Gollancz, 1989.
20 J. Porritt, 'First Moves Toward CFC free Britain', London: *The Times*, 1996, http://media.rsc.org/Climate%20Change/ClCh-pt2.pdf, p.50.
21 J. Button, *How To Be Green*, London: Guild Publishing, 1989.
22 J. Schorsch, 'Are Corporations Playing Clean with Green?', *Business and Society Review*, Autumn 1990, pp. 4–5.
23 D. Kirkpatrick, 'Environmentalism: The New Crusade', *Fortune*, 12 February, 1990, 44–52.
24 F. Cairncross, *Green, Inc.*, London: Earthscan, 1995.
25 The Body Shop, www.thebodyshop.co.uk/_en/_gb/services/aboutus_history.aspx.
26 S. Banerjee, C. S. Gulas and E. Iyer, 'Shades of Green: A Multidimensional Analysis of Environmental Advertising', *Journal of Advertising*, 24(2), 1995, pp. 21–31.
27 Schorsch, 'Are Corporations Playing Clean with Green?', op. cit.

28 M. Lampe and G. M. Gazada, 'Green Marketing in Europe and the United States: An Evolving Business and Society Interface', *International Business Review*, 4(3), 1995, pp. 295–312.
29 EC Environment, 'EU Eco-label', http://ec.europa.eu/environment/ecolabel.
30 History.com, 'Earth Day', www.history.com/topics/earth-day.
31 Rainforest Foundation, 'Who we are', www.rainforestfoundationuk.org/Who_we_are.
32 A. Gajda, 'From Science to Time to Vanity Fair: Sexing up Sustainability and How it Happened', Department of Journalism, University of Illinois, http://gsa.confex.com/gsa/2006AM/finalprogram/abstract_110252.htm.
33 R. Shields, 'It's So Last Year: Vanity Fair Abandons The "Green Issue"', *The Independent*, 5 April 2009, www.independent.co.uk/news/media/its-so-last-year-vanity-fair-abandons-the-green-issue-1662661.html.
34 PIRC, *Climate Safety*, London: Public Interest Research Centre, www.climatesafety.org/download/climatesafety.pdf.
35 *The Independent*, 'Nothing Like a Dame: How Vivienne Westwood Traded a Couture Lifestyle for the Front Line of the Eco War', 12 July 2009, www.independent.co.uk/environment/green-living/nothing-like-a-dame-how-vivienne-westwood-traded-a-couture-lifestyle-for-the-front-line-of-the-eco-war-1739905.html.
36 The Prince of Wales, 'What does The Prince of Wales do to reduce his own carbon footprint?', www.princeofwales.gov.uk/faqs/what_does_the_prince_of_wales_do_to_reduce_his_own_carbon_fo_1742260269.html.
37 Inglehart, R., 2008, Changing Values among Western Publics from 1970 to 2006, *West European Politics* 31(1/2), 2008, pp. 130–46.
38 Lowe, P. P. and Rudig, W., 'Political Ecology and the Social Sciences – The State of the Art', *British Journal of Political Science*, 16, 1986, pp. 513–50.
39 R. E. Dunlap and R. Scarce, 'Environmental Problems and Protection', *Public Opinion Quarterly*, 55(4), 1991, pp. 651–72.
40 G. Smith, 'How Green is My Valley?' *Marketing and Research Today*, June 1990, pp. 76–82.
41 Lampe and Gazada, 'Green Marketing in Europe and the United States: An Evolving Business and Society Interface', op. cit.
42 The Roper Organization report, 'The Environment: Public Attitudes and Individual Behaviour', 1990, quoted in Lampe and Gazada, 'Green Marketing in Europe and the United States: An Evolving Business and Society Interface', op. cit.
43 M. Hulme, *Why We Disagree about Climate Change: Understanding Controversy, Inaction and Opportunity*, Cambridge: Cambridge University Press, 2009.
44 A. Spence, D. Venables, N. Pidgeon, W. Poortinga and C. Demski, *Public Perceptions of Climate Change and Energy Futures in Britain*, Cardiff: Cardiff University, 2010, www.cf.ac.uk/psych/home2/docs/UnderstandingRiskFinalReport.pdf.
45 Eurobarometer, *European Attitudes Towards Climate Change*, Special Report 313, 2009, Brussels: Eurobarometer.
46 M. Holdsworth and P. Steedman, *16 Pain-Free Ways to Save the Planet*, London: National Consumer Council, 2005.
47 Futerra, *Sizzle: The New Climate Message*, London: Futerra Sustainability Communications, 2010.

48 Defra, '2007 Survey of Public Attitudes and Behaviours Towards the Environment', London: Department for Environment, Food and Rural Affairs, *Statistical Release*, 14 August 2007, www.defra.gov.uk/statistics/files/pas2007report.pdf.

7 The future of environmentalism

1 M. Shellenberger and T. Nordhaus, *The Death of Environmentalism: Global Warming Politics in a Post-Environmental World*, Oakland, CA: The Breakthrough Institute, 2004, p. 8, www.thebreakthrough.org/PDF/Death_of_Environmentalism.pdf.
2 A. Evans, *Globalization and Scarcity: Multilateralism for a World With Limits*, New York: Center on International Cooperation, New York University.
3 UNPD, *World Demographic Trends*, New York: United Nations Population Division, 2011.
4 Quoted in N. Robins, 'Making Sustainability Bite: Transforming Global Consumption Patterns', *Journal of Sustainable Product Design*, 10(3), 1999, pp. 7–16.
5 J. Rockström, W. Steffen, K. Noone, A. Persson, F. S. Chapin III, E. F. Lambin, T. M. Lenton, M. Scheffer, C. Folke, H. J. Schellnhuber, B. Nykvist, C. A. de Wit, T. Hughes, S. van der Leeuw, H. Rodhe, S. Sörlin, P. K. Snyder, R. Costanza, U. Svedin, M. Falkenmark, L. Karlberg, R. W. Corell, V. J. Fabry, J. Hansen, B. Walker, D. Liverman, K. Richardson, P. Crutzen and J. A. Foley, 'A Safe Operating Space for Humanity', *Nature* 461, 2009, pp. 472–75, www.nature.com/nature/journal/v461/n7263/full/461472a.html.
6 P. J. Jacques, R. E. Dunlap and M. Freeman, 'The Organisation of Denial: Conservative Think Tanks and Environmental Scepticism', *Environmental Politics*, 17(3), 2008, 349–85, www.informaworld.com/smpp/section?content=a793291693&fulltext=713240928.
7 B. Lomborg, *The Skeptical Environmentalist*, Cambridge: Cambridge University Press, 2001, p. 9.
8 A. M. McCright and R. E. Dunlap, 'Defeating Kyoto: The Conservative Movement's Impact on the U.S. Climate Change Policy', *Social Problems*, 50(3), 2003, pp. 348–73.
9 *The Independent*, 'James Lovelock: Nuclear Power is the Only Green Solution', 24 May 2004, www.ecolo.org/media/articles/articles.in.english/love-indep-24-05-04.htm.
10 G. Monbiot, 'Channel 4's Convenient Green Fictions', *The Guardian*, 4 November 2010, www.guardian.co.uk/commentisfree/cif-green/2010/nov/04/channel-4-convenient-green-fiction.
11 G. Ereaut and N. Segnit, *Warm Words: How We Are Telling the Climate Story and Can We Tell It Better?*, London: IPPR, 2006, p. 7.
12 J. Porritt, *Capitalism As If The Earth Mattered*, London: Earthscan, 2005.
13 T. Crompton and T. Kasser, *Meeting Environmental Challenges: The Role of Human Identity*, Godalming: Worldwide Fund for Nature, 2009, p. 67, www.wwf.org.uk/what_we_do/campaigning/strategies_for_change/?uNews ID=3105.
14 T. Nordhaus and M. Shellenberger, *Break Through: From the Death of Environmentalism to the Politics of Possibility*, New York: Houghton Mifflin, 2007.

15 The Breakthrough Institute, http://thebreakthrough.org/QnA.shtml.
16 Shellenberger and Nordhaus, *The Death of Environmentalism: Global Warming Politics in a Post-Environmental World*, op. cit., p. 3.
17 R. J. Brulle, J. Craig and R. Dunlap, *The Break Through Illusion: A Social Science Critique of Nordhaus and Shellenberger*, Department of Culture Communications, Drexel University: Philadelphia, USA. www.pages.drexel.edu/~brullerj/SN_Critique.pdf.
18 M. Wolf, The Dangers of Living in a Zero-Sum World Economy, *Financial Times*, 19 December 2007, www.ft.com/cms/s/0/0447f562-ad85-11dc-9386-0000779fd2ac.html#axzz1LYgj5PUy.
19 C. Snell and C. Quinn, 'International Development and Global Poverty', in T. Fitzpatrick, *Understanding the Environment and Social Policy*, Bristol: The Policy Press, 2011, pp. 291–311.
20 R. Wilkinson and K. Pickett, *The Spirit Level: Why Equal Societies Almost Always Do Better*, London: Allen Lane, 2009.

Further reading

1 Some books that provide further historical information

R. D. Bullard, *Confronting Environmental Racism: Voices from the Grassroots*, Cambridge: South End Press, 1993.

J. R. McNeill, *Something New Under the Sun: An Environmental History of the World in the 20th Century*, Harmondsworth: Penguin, 2000.

J. Radku, translated by T. Dunlap, *Nature and Power: A Global History of the Environment*, Cambridge: Cambridge University Press, 1998.

D. Richardson and C. Rootes, *The Green Challenge: The Development of Green Parties in Europe*, London: Routledge, 1995.

R. W. Righter, *The Battle over Hetch Hetchy: America's Most Controversial Dam and the Birth of Modern Environmentalism*, Oxford: Oxford University Press, 2005.

H. Ritvo, *Dawn of Green: Manchester, Thirlmere and Modern Environmentalism*, Chicago: Chicago University Press, 2009.

E. Russell, *War and Nature: Fighting Humans and Insects with Chemicals from World War I to Silent Spring*, Cambridge: Cambridge University Press, 2001.

D. Worster, *Nature's Economy: A History of Ecological Ideas*, Cambridge: Cambridge University Press, 1998.

2 Some books that deal with contemporary environmental issues and debates

F. Ackerman, *Can We Afford the Future? The Economics of a Warming World*, London: Zed Books, 2009.

J. Hannigan, *Environmental Sociology*, 2nd edn, London: Routledge, 2006.

M. Hulme, *Why We Disagree about Climate Change: Understanding Controversy, Inaction and Opportunity*, Cambridge: Cambridge University Press, 2009.

B. Lomborg, *The Skeptical Environmentalist*, Cambridge: Cambridge University Press, 2001.

T. Nordhaus and M. Shellenberger, *Break Through: From the Death of Environmentalism to the Politics of Possibility*, New York: Houghton Mifflin, 2007.

N. Schrijver, J. Crawford and S. Panitchpakdi, *Development without Destruction: The UN and Global Resource Management*, Bloomington: Indiana University Press, 2010.
L. Swart and E. Perry (eds), *Global Environmental Governance: Perspectives on the Current Debate*, New York: Center for UN Reform Education, 2007.
E. O. Wilson, *The Diversity of Life*, new edn, London: Penguin, 2001.
S. Yearley, *Cultures of Environmentalism: Empirical Studies in Environmental Sociology*, Basingstoke: Palgrave Macmillan, 2005.

Index

10:10 campaign 85
11th Hour, The 85
'50 Years is Enough' campaign 16
9/11 terrorist attacks 17

'A Blueprint for Survival' (*The Economist*) 3
acid rain 49–51, 56, 57
'Act on CO_2' campaign 80
advertising, commercial 76–77, 82
Aerosol Connection, The (FoE UK) 81
Afton, North Carolina 14
Age of Stupid, The 85
Agenda 21 32–33
Alliance of Small Islands 38
Amazon river 20
Amchitka Island 12
American Electric Power 20
American Power Act 22–23
American Recovery and Reinvestment Act (2009) 71
American Students for a Democratic Society 7
Amis de la Terre, Les 9
animal testing 81
Antarctic 35, 81
anti-consumerism 16–17
anti-environment movement 94–95
anti-globalisation campaigns 5, 17
anti-nuclear movement 2, 4, 7, 10–11, 12, 13
anti-roads campaigns 15, 16
anti-whaling campaigns 12–13, 82
apartheid 81
Apollo 8 78
Apollo 11 77

Apple 19
'Are you doing your bit?' campaign 80
Aristotle 41
Armstrong, Franny 85
atomic energy 28
Atomic Energy Commission 8
Attenborough, David 83–84
Audubon, John James 6
Avaaz 23

baby milk 81
Barbier, Edward B. 71–72
Barclays Bank 81
Basel Convention 35
Bayer 19
BBC 76, 86
beauty products 82
Beaver Committee Report (1954) 50, 66
behaviour, and environmental attitudes 91, 96–97
Bellamy, David 83
Benetton 81
Berkeley, California 79
Big Ask campaign 21–22
Billner, Börje 28
biodiversity 48, 49, 92, 94
biodiversity hotspot 106 n14
biodiversity loss 48, 49
bioeconomic programme 64
Biosphere Conference (1968) 27
Body Shop, The 82
Bolivia 20
Bookchin, Murray 46, 106 n10
Botanic Gardens Conservation International 20

bottle banks 79–80
Bottle Bill (Oregon) 79
bottles, non-returnable 9, 79
Boulding, Kenneth E. 62, 64
bovine spongiform encephalopathy (BSE) 52
boycotting 81
BP 20, 68
Brand, Stewart 95
Brandt Report 30, 32
Brandt, Willy 30
Brazil 26, 29, 38, 40, 72
Brazilian Amazonas 84
Brent Spar oil platform 53–54
British Antarctic Survey 35
British Ecological Society 42
British Gas 80
British Rail 80
British Telecom 20, 80
Brower, David 61
Brown, Gordon 71
Brulle, R. J. 100 n3
Brundtland, Gro Harlem 31, 92
Brundtland Report 31
Bulgaria 88
Bulova 76
Bündnis 90/Die Grünen 10
Burke, Tom 9
Bush, George H. 32, 51
Bush, George W. 33
Buy Nothing Day 16

Californian Fisheries and Game Department 44
Campaign for Better Transport 22
Campaign for Nuclear Disarmament (CND) 11
Campaign to Protect Rural England (CPRE) 6, 15
Canada 50, 83
'cap-and-trade' system 23
capitalist system, reforming 99
car ownership 76
carbon dioxide emissions 37, 88, 93; reducing 40; targets 39
carbon footprint 83, 88, 93
carbon trading scheme 68
Carson, Rachel 3, 8, 41, 44–45
Cartagena Protocol 35
Charles, Prince of Wales 86

Chernobyl 11, 31, 87
China 26, 27, 37, 38, 39, 40, 71, 72
chlorofluorocarbon (CFC) 35–36, 81
Clean Air Act (UK) 50
Clean Air Act (US) 8, 76
Clean Community System (California) 79
Clean Development Mechanism 68
Clean Water Act (US) 8
Clear Lake 44
Climate Camp 22
climate change 17, 20–24, 26, 33, 40, 47, 57, 92, 94–96, 98–99; and depletion of ozone layer 35–36; economics of 67–68; European Union 88; Friends of the Earth 21–22; global policy 36–39; Greenpeace 22; individual responsibility 89–90; popular culture 84–85; and public interest 88–89; research into 48–49; scepticism of 56, 94; United Kingdom 88–89; United States 89
Climate Change Act (2008) 21
Climate Change Bill (2010) 22–23
Climate Research Unit (CRU) 55–56
Climate Safety (Public Interest Research Centre) 85
climate science 48–49, 53, 54–57, 67, 88
Clinton, Bill 14
Clooney, George 84
Club of Rome 63
Coalition Against Runway 2 (CAR2) 22
Cobb, John B. 65
Coca Cola 19
Cochabamba, Bolivia 70
Cohn-Bendit, Daniel 10
Commission of Sustainable Development (CSD) 32
Committee on Climate Change 21
Common Crisis North-South: Cooperation for World Recovery (Brandt Commission) 30, 31
Commoner, Barry 62
community obligation 70
Conference of the Parties (COP) 37–39
conservation biology 48

Conservation International 20
Conservative Government (UK) 15
consumer awareness 81–82
consumerism 73, 75–77, 80–81, 91
consumption 32, 63, 64, 73, 76–77, 80, 83, 86, 89–90, 93, 98, 99
Convention on Biological Diversity (CBD) 32, 48, 49
Convention on International Trade in Endangered Species of Wild Fauna and Flora 35
Copenhagen Accord 38–39
cost-benefit analysis 66, 68
Costanza, Robert 65, 67
Council for the Preservation of Rural England (CPRE) 6
Cousteau, Jacques 83
Crompton, Tom 96–97
Crying Indian campaign 79
Cuyahoga River 77
Czech Republic 9

Daily Mirror 12
Daily Telegraph, The 56
Daly, Herman E. 64, 65
Darwin, Charles 42
Day After Tomorrow, The 85
decentralisation 99
decoupling 73
deep ecology 46
Deepwater Horizon 23, 68
Defenders of Wildlife 6
deforestation 39
Dell 19
Department for the Environment (UK) 47, 51
Department for Transport 16
development 29–31
Development Alternatives 93
DiCaprio, Leonardo 85
dichlorodiphenyldichloroethane (DDD) 44
dichlorodiphenyltrichloroethane (DDT) 8, 41
discount rates 67–68
Don't Make a Wave Committee 12
Duchy Originals 86
Dutilleux, Jean-Pierre 84

Eagle lunar module 77
Earth: biocapacity 93; from space 78
Earth Action Network 82
Earth Day 1, 78–79, 87
Earth Day: A Question of Survival (CBS) 78
Earth First! 14, 16
Earth Summit; Rio 31–34, 38, 49, 94; Stockholm 40
Earthrise 78
Earthwatch 20
East Germany 29
Ecolabel 82–83
ecological footprint 65
ecological overshoot 93–94
Ecological Society of America 43
Ecologist, The 45
ecology 56; age of 100 n6; use of term 42
Ecology Center 79
Ecology Party 11
economic development 26, 28, 33, 39, 98
economic growth 10, 31, 33–34, 37, 46, 58, 59–65, 72–73, 75, 95
economic value of nature 65–68
economy, sustainable 97
ecosystem services approach 67, 69
EDF 82
Ehrlich, Paul 28, 61, 62, 63–64, 66
Elkington, John 81
Emerson, Ralph Waldo 100 n4
Endangered Species Act 8
energy security 80, 98–99
energy use 80
England 88
environment, use of term 1–2
environmental attitudes 89–90; and behaviour 91, 96–97
Environmental Defense Fund (EDF) 7, 8
environmental justice 13–15, 16
Environmental Protection Agency (US) 35, 47, 66
ethical investment 81–83
European Recovery Program (US) 60, 75
European Union (EU) 38, 40, 71; climate change, attitudes to 88; genetically modified (GM) food/

Index   119

crops 52; green labelling 83;
    Parliamentary Elections 1989 11
Exxon Mobil 55
Exxon Valdez 87

fashion industry 85–86
Financial Times 98
Finland 9
Fischer, Joschka 10
fish/fisheries 27, 43, 47, 50, 51, 70,
    72, 77
Food and Agricultural Organization
    (FAO) 29
Food and Drink Administration
    (FDA) 52
food security/safety 59–60, 67, 70,
    98–99; *see also* genetically
    modified (GM) food/crops
forests/forestry 5, 13, 27, 32, 37, 39,
    43, 47, 50, 51, 72, 85, 93; carbon
    projects 20–21, 68
Fortune 82
Forum for the Future 20
fossil fuels 64, 71, 72
*Founex Report on Development and
    Environment, The* (UN) 28
France 7, 9, 83
French Intelligence Agency 13
Friends of the Earth (FoE) 7, 8, 9,
    11; anti-roads campaigns 15, 16;
    The Big Ask campaign 21–22;
    climate change 21–22
Friends of the Earth (FoE) UK 9
Friends of the Earth International
    99
fuel efficiency 59

G8 summit, Birmingham 16–17;
    Genoa 5
G20 summit, London 71; Pittsburgh
    71–72
G77/China grouping 27
Gaia hypothesis 46–47, 95
Galbraith, John Kenneth 61, 77
genetically modified (GM) food/
    crops 49, 51–53, 56, 95
genuine progress indicator 65
Georgescu-Roegen, Nicholas 64, 66
Germany 51, 80
Getting Nowhere Fast (FoE) 15

glacial melt 56
Glass Manufacturers' Federation 80
Global Atmosphere Research
    Programme (GARP) 48
Global Biodiversity Outlook (2010) 49
Global Climate Coalition 21, 55
Global Environment Facility (GEF)
    32
Global Environment Monitoring
    System (GEMS) 48
Global Green New Deal (GGND)
    70–72
Global Street Party 17
global warming *see* climate
    change
Global Witness 15
globalisation 1, 17, 34, 92, 93
Goldsmith, Edward 45
Gorbachev, Mikhail 10
Gore, Al 84, 85
grebes 44
Green Climate Fund 39
Green Consumer Guide, The
    (Elkington and Hailes) 81
Green economy budget 71
Green League, *Vihreä liitto*
    (Finland) 9
green labelling 82–83
green lifestyles 91
green localism 99
Green My Apple 19
Green Party (Germany) 10, 80
Green Party of England and Wales
    10–11, 15
green stimulus investment 71
Greenham Common Air Force
    Base 14
Greenpeace 1, 7, 11, 16, 45, 102 n35;
    anti-consumerism 16–17; anti-
    nuclear campaigns 12; anti-roads
    campaigns 14; anti-whaling
    campaigns 12–13, 82; Brent Spar
    oil platform campaign 53–54;
    climate change 22; Noel Kampff
    Climate Action Project
    investigation 20–21; organisation
    of 19
Greenpeace International 19
Greenpeace (ship) 12
greenwash 79, 82

gross domestic product (GDP) 65, 70–71, 72
gross national product (GNP) 62–63
Gulf of Mexico 23, 68

Haeckel, Ernst 42
Hailes, Julia 81
Hannigan, John 100 n3, 106 n12
happy planet index 65
Hardin, Garrett 3, 69, 70
Harvey, Harold 106 n20
Hetch Hetchy Valley 6
Hindmarch, Anya 1, 86
Hippocrates 3, 41
Holdren, John P. 62, 66
Hoyle, Fred 78
HSBC 20
human activity, impact of 93–94
human identity 96–97
human rights 13
Humboldt, Alexander von 42
Hungary 9
Hurricane Katrina 84
Huxley, Julian 11

Inconvenient Truth, An 85
index of sustainable economic welfare 65
India 26, 32, 38, 40, 65
Inglehart, Ronald 87
'Inimical Effects on Wildlife of periodic DDD Applications to Clear Lake' (Hunt and Bischoff) 44
Interfaith Power and Light 23
International Bank for Reconstruction and Development *see* World Bank
International Conference on Water and the Environment (1992) 69
international development 13
International Monetary Fund (IMF) 16, 30, 60
International Panel on Climate Change (IPCC) 36–37, 38, 54–56; Working Group 1, 48
International Union for Conservation of Nature (IUCN) 48, 106 n14
International Whaling Commission 13

internet activism 17, 19, 23, 55, 56, 57, 99
IPAT equation 62
Ireland 88
Italy 83
ITV 76
Izaak Walton League 6, 8

Jackson, Tim 73
Japan 40
Jevons, William Stanley 59
Johannesburg Declaration on Sustainable Development 34
Journal of Retailing 76

Kalm, Pehr 42
Kasser, Tim 96–97
Keep America Beautiful (KAB) 79
Kelly, Petra 10
Kennedy, John F. 45
Kennedy, Robert F. 62–63
Kennedy, Robert, Jr 84
Kenya 29
Khosla, Ashok 93
Kids Against Pollution 82
King, Alexander 63
Kropotkin, Peter 42
Kyoto Protocol 33, 37–38, 39, 68

Labour Government (UK) 16
Lalonde, Brice 9
land economics 58–59
Lebow, Victor 76–77
Leibovitz, Annie 84
Leopold, Aldo 43
Life 8
Life on Earth 83–84
Limits to Growth (Club of Rome; Meadows, *et al*) 3, 28, 63
Linnaeus, Carl 42, 48
Lithuania 88
litter 79
Live Aid 84
Live Earth 85
Lomborg, Bjørn 55, 94–95
London smog 50
London Heathrow: third runway 22, 66
Love Canal, New York State 14
Lovelock, James 46–47, 95

low carbon 71, 72, 88
Lucas, Caroline 11

M11 link, London 16
M17, Glasgow 15–16
Malaysia 32
Malthus, Thomas 42, 59, 61
Manchester 50; International Airport 22
Man's Impact on the Global Environment: Assessment and Recommendations for Action (MIT) 66
Marks 76
Marx, Karl 59
Massachusetts Institute of Technology (MIT) 63, 66
McDonald's 19, 82
McGraw, Ali 84
McNamara, Robert 30
metals 63–64
Metcalfe, Ben 45
Metuktire, Raoni 84
Mexico 65
Miljöpartiet de gröna 9
Mill, John Stuart 59–61, 65
Millennium Development Goals (MDGs) 34
Millennium Ecosystem Assessment 66–67
molecular biology 52
Monsanto 19
Montreal Protocol on Substances that Deplete the Ozone Layer 35–36, 81
Moore, Norman 44
Morales, Evo 70
Mororua Atoll 13
Mouvement d'Ecologie Politique 9
MoveOn 23
Muir, John 6, 101 n4
multilateral environmental agreements (MEAs) 26–27, 34–36, 37
Myers, Norman 106 n14

Nader, Ralph 76
Naess, Arne 46
National Aeronautics and Space Administration (NASA) 46

National Audubon Society 6, 8
national economic competition 40
National Environmental Policy Act 8
National Traffic and Motor Vehicle Safety Act 76
National Trust 6, 19, 22
National Wildlife Federation 6, 8, 19
Natural Resources Defense Council (NRDC) 1, 7, 19
Nature 94
Nature Conservancy 12, 20; Toxic Chemicals and Wildlife research station 44
negative externalities 60, 67
Nelson, Gaylord 78
Nestlé 19, 81
net positive impact initiative 68
Netherlands 88–89
New Deal 70, 71
New Left (France) 7
New Partnership for Africa's Development (NEPAD) 34
New Zealand 83
Newbury bypass 16
Newman, Paul 84
NGO Global Forum 32, 33
Nicholson, Max 12
Nimbus Earth observation satellites 48
nitrogen 94
Nixon, Richard 61, 78
no net loss initiative 68
Noel Kampff Climate Action Project 20–21
Nordhaus, Ted 97–98
Nordhaus, William 68
North America 50
North-South: A Program for Survival (Brandt Commission) 30
North-South Summit 30
nuclear energy 11, 57, 95; *see also* anti-nuclear movement

Obama, Barack 22, 38
oil spills 3–4, 23, 53–54, 68, 77, 87
Organisation for Economic Co-operation and Development (OECD) 50

Organization of the Petroleum Exporting Countries (OPEC) 80
Osborn, Henry Fairfield, Jr 61
Ostrom, Elinor 70
Our Common Future (Brundtland Report) 31, 92
ozone hole, Antarctic 81, 87
ozone layer 57; depletion of 35–36, 81

Pacificorp 20
Paley Commission 61
Paley, William 61
palm oil 20
Parkin, Sara 11
peal oil 23
Pearson Commission 32
Peccei, Aurelio 63
People Party 11
pesticides, chemical 43–45, 57
Pigou, Arthur C. 60, 67
Plane Stupid 22
planetary boundaries 94
Pliny the Elder 41
Poland 9
politics of possibility 97–98
pollution 3–4, 8, 14–15, 69, 79, 82, 87, 89, 94; air 50, 66; and income 15; noise 66; oil 3–4, 23, 53–54, 68, 77, 87; vehicle 76
Pond, Walden 42
Population Bomb, The (Ehrlich) 28
population growth 59, 61, 62–64, 92
Porritt, Jonathon 81
post-materialism 87–89
Postlethwaite, Pete 85
poverty 92, 93; eradication of 33–34, 37, 39, 70, 72–73, 98
Powell, Colin 33–34
Problems of the Human Environment (UN) 27–28
public interest 24, 87–89
public service 66–67

Race, Stanley 80
racial discrimination 14–15
Rainbow Warrior 13
Rainforest Foundation International 84
Ramsar Convention 35

Ray, John 42
Reader's Digest 8
Reclaim the Streets 16
recycling 79–80, 82, 83
Red Data Books 48, 106 n14
Reagan, Ronald 51, 80
resources, natural 15, 27–28, 30, 32, 43, 91, 93; conservation of 79; and the economy 58–59, 61–64; efficient use of 75; limits to 42, 45–46, 63, 75; privatising 68–70; renewable 71, 73, 93
'Revolt of the Bird watchers' (Associated Press) 8, 101 n12
Rhine River 31
Ricardo, David 59
Rio Declaration on Environment and Development 32
Rio Grande river 20
roads 13–14, 15–16, 76
Roads for Prosperity (UK White Paper) 15
Roberts, Julia 84
Roddick, Anita 82
Romania 88
Roosevelt, Franklin D. 70
Roskill Commission 66
Rotterdam Convention 35
Royal Commission for Environment Pollution 47
Royal Society 55, 56
Royal Society for the Protection of Birds (RSPB) 6, 7, 19, 22, 101 n10
Royal Train 86
Russell, Muir 56

Sainsbury's 86
Santa Barbara Channel 77
'Save It' campaign 80
Save the Whale 12–13, 82
Scandinavia 50
Schumacher, E. F. 3, 64
Schweppes 9
Science Advisory Committee 45
Sears, Paul 46
Seeger, Peter 84
'selling the sausage' approach 90
Shell 54
Shellenberger, Michael 97–98
Sierra Club 6, 7, 8, 61, 101 n9

Silent Spring (Carson) 3, 8, 41
Simon, Julian 63–64
Singer, Fred 55
Sizzle: The New Climate Message (Futerra) 90
Slovenia 88
Smith, Adam 58–59
Smith, Robert Angus 50
social equity 31
Society for the Promotion of Nature Reserves 6
Society for the Protection of Ancient Buildings 22
socio-economic development 33
South Korea 71
South Yorkshire County Council 80
Soviet bloc 26, 28; *see also* individual countries
spaceship Earth 62, 64
Sports Illustrated 8
Starbucks 20
Statement of Forest Principles 32
steady-state economy (SSE) 65
Stern, Nicholas 67–68
Stern Review (2006) 67–68
Sting 84
Stockholm Convention 35
Stop Climate Chaos coalition 22
Strong, Maurice 32
student protests 7, 10
Styler, Trudy 84
substantial equivalence 52
Sukhdev, Pavan 72
sulphur dioxide 50–51
Superfund (1980) 14
sustainable development 31–34, 65, 72, 74
Sweden 9, 28, 50, 88

television 76–77
Tesco 20, 80, 83
Thant (UN Secretary General) 27
Thatcher, Margaret 15, 80
Theophrastus 41
thermodynamics, second law of 64
Thirlmere reservoir 6
This Common Inheritance (UK Government) 15
Thoreau, Henry 42, 100 n4
Time 87

Times, The (UK) 52–53
Torrey Canyon 3
trade protectionism 17
'tragedy of the commons' 69
Transition Towns movement 23
Transport Reform Group 15
travel, international 77
Truman, Harry S. 27, 61
Turgot, Anne-Robert-Jacques 59
Turkey 88
Twyford Down 15, 16
Type I and Type II Partnerships 34

Undersea World of Jacques Cousteau, The 83
Unilever 20
Union Carbide 31, 87
Union Oil Company 3
United Church of Christ's Commission for Racial Justice 14
United Kingdom: acid rain 50, 51; climate change, attitudes to 88–89; climate science 56; genetically modified (GM) food/crops 52–53
United Nations 27, 31, 48, 92
United Nations Conference on Environment and Development (UNCED) *see* Earth Summit: Rio
United Nations Conference on the Conservation and Utilization of Resources (UNSCCUR) 27
United Nations Conference on the Human Environment (UNCHE) 1, 26, 28–29, 31, 38, 50
United Nations Declaration on Permanent Sovereignty over Natural Resources 27
United Nations Economic and Social Council 27, 29
United Nations Educational, Scientific and Cultural Organization (UNESCO) 11, 27
United Nations Environment Programme (UNEP) 29, 36, 40, 68, 70, 72
United Nations Framework Convention on Climate Change (UNFCCC) 32, 35, 36, 37, 39, 49

United Nations General Assembly 29; Resolution (1966) 27; Resolution 2398(XXIII) 28; Resolution 38/161 31; Resolution 55/199 33; Resolution S-19/2 33
United States 38, 40, 71; acid rain 51; chemical pesticides 43–45; chlorofluorocarbon (CFC) 36; climate change, attitudes to 89; climate science 56; conservative movement 94; economy 32, 33, 38, 60–61; genetically modified (GM) food/crops 52–53; green labelling 83
University of East Anglia (UEA) 55–56
Unsafe at Any Speed 76

Valley of the Drums, Kentucky 14
valleys, damming of 6
Vanity Fair 84
Vienna Convention for the Protection of Ozone Layer 35

Wall Street Journal, The 55
Walmart 20
Waring, Marilyn 65
water, privatisation of 69–70
Weber, Max 3
WEHAB 34
Westwood, Vivienne 85–86
whaling 12–13
Wheeler, Elmer 90
Wilderness Society 6
Wildlife Trust 6

Wilson, E. O. 56
Wise Use Movement 21
Wolf, Martin 98
Woodbury, New Jersey 79
Wordsworth, William 100 n4
World Bank 16, 30, 32, 60, 65, 69, 72
World Climate Research Programme 48
World Commission on Environment and Development (WCED) 31
World Conservation Strategy (IUCN) 31
world environment organisation 40
World Health Organisation (WHO) 29
World Meteorological Organization (WMO) 29, 36
World Social Forum 17
World Summit on Sustainable Development (WSSD) 33–34
World Trade Organization (WTO) 16, 17, 52
World Values Survey 100 n1
World Wildlife Fund (WWF) 7, 11, 12, 20, 93, 101 n11
World Wildlife Fund for Nature 7
World Wildlife Fund International 20
Worldchanging 96
Worster, Donald 100 n6

Yale University 89
Yangtze river 20
Yorke, Thom 21